ADVANCE PRAISE

Jill has guided me through four C-suite transitions over the past 10+ years. She is one of my trusted advisors and the first person I call when I hit a leadership road block. Jill's book is a must read for practical in the moment advice for anything from leading a large transformation to making it through a challenging day at the office. I'm thrilled the world gets to benefit from all this wisdom that I used to lead every day. Buy the book, go hear her speak and if your fortunate enough to get on her calendar, hire her to be your coach!

–*Peter Walker*
CFO & EVP Sterling Talent Solutions

From the moment you meet Jill, or Coach J. as I call her, you know you're in the presence of an exceptional human being. It is her clear confidence and comfort in her own skin that makes her a tremendous thought partner, guide and coach. Jill helped me navigate a difficult transition back to work after my first child; I was headed for a cliff. With such simple, clear and thoughtful guidance, she shifted my perspective entirely. And suddenly the world was full of possibility. Jill lives in a world of possibility, of opportunity and positivity – she helped me see that at every opportunity I had a choice – the choice to be my highest, best self. It changed everything.

–*Avina Gupta, PhD*
Leadership Development, Chick-fil-A

Through her 30-year career as a senior HR executive and coach, Jill has pretty much seen it all, advising countless leaders of all levels on how to up their game, even in the face of obstacles and challenges. Her no nonsense style is inspiring and empowering, and yet practical and doable. I know because I've been a lucky beneficiary of her life and leadership wisdom for over two decades.

Through real-world, relatable examples from Jill's treasure trove of experience, Through Trust and Collaboration is a must read for any HR professional who wants a proven roadmap to help develop resilient leaders and corporate cultures that drive high impact results!

–*Jennifer Hale*
CEO, Speaker & Coach, The Hale Group
Former SVP People & Culture, Assurant

As an executive, it is a daily occurrence to juggle and stretch to perform at the highest levels. I was fortunate to meet Jill through a "high potential" program that paths executives to the C-suite. Until that time, I found myself working incredibly hard and the work was often tiring; While finding professional success, I found the energy it took to support my career and family priorities drained me at the end of each day.

By working with Jill, I found work more enjoyable and learned how to protect time for what was most important. Through her mentorship, we unlocked my true potential. I don't work any less today than before our coaching, but I am able to balance the duties to enjoy the work I do and come home with more energy to spend time with my family.

Jill's leadership coaching is the best investment anyone could make in their career. She is a brilliant executive "whisperer" that advises with the most authentic spirit. She works with purpose and it shows. Read her book and you will begin to see that you are always "in choice".

–Angela Navarro
President & Chief Operating Officer, Beecher Reagan

I have had the privilege of working with, or directly for, Jill for thirteen years. As a result, I received routine/timely feedback and coaching which ultimately helped me become a more effective leader, and more importantly, a better person overall. And, I have seen other leaders who heeded Jill's advice along the way become more impactful and effective too. The book is full of the same wisdom and advice I received from Jill every day. It is like having a reference manual to help me recall our regular talks and a constant reminder about the value of "keeping things simple" now that we no longer working together.

–*Jack Buehler*
SVP, Human Resources

A life changing read for anyone and everyone who strives to be an effective leader at the highest levels. Jill gives us the gift of practical, in the moment tools to help us navigate through an unpredictable and ever changing world with optimism and confidence.

–*Dorsey Levens*
Running Back (retired)
Green Bay Packers – Hall of Fame
Leadership and Mental Toughness Coach

In just a few short months, Jill has helped me to unravel some of the stories that I've been telling myself for too many years and has reminded me to stayed focused on my successes and my strengths. She has given me great tools that make me more aware of my energy and how it affects those around me. It's already helped me with some difficult relationships both at work and at home. Can't wait to see where it takes me! I highly recommend her book as a great place to start.

–Kristen McGuffey
Executive Vice President &
General Counsel, Serta Simmons

Jill Ratliff is the real deal. Now there's finally a book on leadership that provides simple concepts that when put into practice will truly unleash extraordinary results. If you're ready to be the leader (and the person!) you've always wanted to be – not just in the easy times, but in those high-intensity, critical moments – you must read this book! I've found there are opportunities to practice these skills every day – and it is life-changing.

–Libby Pollack
Global Change and Strategy
Habitat for Humanity International

Jill gave me back my power. Her guidance led me to a place of peace, trust and confidence. Jill brings you back to believing in YOU. She reminds you that regardless of your success so far, you can keep get better.

We all feel overworked, underappreciated and over-whelmed at times. The concept of work-life balance often didn't seem realistic, but through Jill's work, she helps you bring "true" balance back to your life. She teaches you how to use the tools you already have and she brings out the best in you and helps you un-tap your full potential. Her book opens the door to a new way of thinking.

Jill was a game changer for me. She helped me grow to become the leader (and wife, mother, and friend) I didn't know I could be.

–Gabrielle Dow
Vice President, Marketing
Green Bay Packers

This book is for everyone. Whether you are leading Human Capital, leading people or simply leading your-self through life, there are wonderful nuggets of wisdom included here. While Jill focuses on the HR professional, her advice and approach is applicable to everyone both in the office and at home! A quick read. Not since the "One Minute Manager" have we had a book so simple to understand and so easy to implement.

–Mary McCoy
Leadership Development Consultant
Retired Hewlett Packard Executive

For Jill, finding JOY is her priority and negativity cannot exist. She's shown me how to incorporate those princi-ples in my life. The tools she teaches show you how to adjust in the moment and in the face of life's challenges; Seeing them as golden opportunities to learn something valuable. I find that kind of tolerance and ability to pivot is the epicenter of leadership success. She is the most gifted person I know at teaching how to adjust your own lens to practice these life-serving skills. Jill helps you find your most powerful place again and again.

–Ann McDonald
Morris, Manning, & Martin LLP

Jill's work delivers a path for leaders to be genuinely authentic versions of themselves. When we focus on responding, not reacting, to colleagues and our teams with respect for their perspective and with commitment to the mission of the organization/ team/ project we are truly leaders. Learning how to lead yourself first is the key to engaging with colleagues, and achieves the best results for our teams and our organizations. Her book provides an elegant framework for how to start this leadership journey.

–Kathleen Brown
Senior Vice President, Innovation
ClearBalance

Jill and her coaching has helped transform my presence and leadership in my business and my home. Now, more often than not, I am able to pause, reflect, and respond in a way that is both productive and positive allowing for potentially negative interactions to become growth situations. I couldn't more highly recommend this book or her executive coaching.

–Brett Bronson
O/O, McDonald's Corp

Jill's coaching is exactly what I needed to break through the ceiling I had created for myself and achieve the next level, not only in my career but in life. Simply learning about the balance of power and how to remain in it was a total game changer for me. Not only am I able to remain in my power, I am able to identify when others aren't, and respond to situations in a way that does not escalate the tension. People are naturally drawn to consistent and steadfast leaders, especially amidst a storm. What I have gained through working with Jill has elevated the influence I have across my teams, organization, and both personal and professional networks. I apply it every day, in every aspect of my life. Read her book, it's like have a cup coffee with her and gaining her wisdom and insight.

–Jennifer Joiner
Transformation Consultant, North Highland

I remember my first meeting with Jill Ratliff. She told me "don't do anything drastic. Let me teach you some tools to manage your daily stress. You'll feel entirely different in 6 months". As a competitive, driven executive who struggled to balance work, travel, a duel career family and two small children, I found myself focusing on everyone except myself. As a result, I was overwhelmed and unhappy.

She was right. Now, months later, I feel different and perform at a higher level. Jill gave me what I needed, the actual tools and tangible exercises, instead of personal development theories. Read her book, you will begin to understand it's not as hard as we're making it!

–Allison Kline
Senior Director, Cox

LEADERSHIP THROUGH TRUST & COLLABORATION

LEADERSHIP THROUGH TRUST & COLLABORATION

Practical Tools for Today's Results-Driven Leader

JILL RATLIFF

NEW YORK

LONDON • NASHVILLE • MELBOURNE • VANCOUVER

Leadership Through Trust & Collaboration

Practical Tools for Today's Results-Driven Leader

Published in New York, New York, by Mount Tabor Media a branded imprint of Morgan James Publishing in partnership with Difference Press. Morgan James is a trademark of Morgan James, LLC. www.MorganJamesPublishing.com

ISBN 9781642798593 paperback
ISBN 9781642798609 eBook
Library of Congress Control Number: 2019951760

Cover Design Concept:
MVO Marketing

Cover & Interior Design by:
Christopher Kirk
www.GFSstudio.com

Editor:
Todd Hunter

Book Coaching:
The Author Incubator

TABLE OF CONTENTS

FOREWORD

If we're lucky, people come into our lives and tell us what we need to hear when we need to hear it. Their words come from a depth of experience combined with a bold sense of caring. I'm one of the lucky ones, and Jill Ratliff has time and again had the courage and wisdom to be one of those people for me.

I bought a small leadership development firm more than 15 years ago, taking a big step away from a career I knew and into an industry, function, and practice that I did not. Jill, a senior HR executive and someone I knew (although not well), was one of the first people I reached out to invite to join an advisory board for my small firm with a big vision. In our first meeting, over lunch at a Mexican restaurant, and not yet beyond the chips and salsa, Jill said, "So, your first challenge is that you look young. We've got to work on getting others to believe that you're battle-tested enough to develop their top talent."

Of course, she was right. And, lucky for me, she was also immediately 'all in' in helping us to build our credibility, our skill sets, and our firm to have the sort of impact that we knew it could. She saw potential, she recognized passion, and she helped me believe in myself. Fast forward, and since that lunch we have grown the firm by more than 5X and have had the privilege to support the development of thousands of high-potential, high-performing women and men in more than 400 organizations. And, in each large-scale program, Jill Ratliff is there – sharing her gifts by facilitating workshops, personally engaging in mentoring, and continually challenging both me and the firm to do and achieve more.

Jill believes that moments matter in leadership, yet many in leadership roles wait for difficult moments to pass or miss those moments that have real meaning. *Leadership through Trust & Collaboration* provides a lens through which to see the present, and to be present – recognizing how you're showing up in the world and seeing the value of leaning forward into opportunities to grow. The examples and stories herein are both inspiring and practical, with alchemy and simplicity.

There are thousands of books written every year on leadership in business; but few combine a depth of experience with a bold sense of caring. In these pages, you will experience Jill Ratliff as senior executive, trusted advisor, executive coach, speaker, leader, mother, sister, and friend. You will benefit from perspectives taken from high-pressure situations at the top of the house in some of our largest corporations as well as those taken from a loved one's bedside. And, you will benefit from how the perspectives masterfully intertwine to help each of us better understand the 'human operating system' and our roles as leaders.

The good news is, it's no longer questioned if I'm sufficiently battle-tested to develop top talent. I'm still learning every day, but I'm far more attuned to the power of words borne from a depth of experience and a bold sense of caring.

Helene Lollis
President & CEO
Pathbuilders, Inc.
*"Advancing Leadership Development &
Gender Diversity"*

INTRODUCTION

I f you are reading this book you are someone who cares about developing leaders and teams that can achieve their full potential. You have committed yourself to doing just that. You're responsible for being the "keeper" of people and culture initiatives for your organization, or you are a leader who wants to be the kind of leader that people trust and want to follow. You care about growing people as well as the business because you know that one is the fuel that produces the bottom line for the other.

You are passionate about your work and have invested a great amount of time figuring out the best way to help your CEO and your leaders grow. Sometimes you may feel that you care about it more than they do. You probably do. That's OK. It's your job and that's why they need you.

Most CEOs and leaders want to be great. But they don't have time to read and digest all the books, attend all of the workshops, and study all of the things that great leaders do. They're busy running the business, and for the most part, they're doing a pretty dang good job at it.

The truth is, for so many leaders, it would be enough if we could only figure out how to help them be their best self every day, in any situation, and not get tripped up by that one weakness, trait, or quality that gets in their way, the blind spot that they can't see or figure out how to change, the one piece of "behavioral feedback" that follows them around on all of their 360 assessments. It usually gets attributed to the derailers in their personality assessments. You know, it's the downside to their upsides.

What if it really doesn't have anything to do with problems in someone's personality? What if it has to do with simply being human and never having learned exactly how to navigate the harder parts of that, both for ourselves as leaders and for the people we lead? What if, instead of thinking that we all have "personality flaws," it's really just simple leadership skills and practices which, if they knew how, could close the gap and free leaders from overanalyzing themselves and everyone else so they could just do what they do best and enjoy being a leader?

Trust

If we know that great cultures attract great people and great people want to work for leaders they admire and trust, then we need to make sure we understand what gets in the way of building trust. You already know this, no doubt. It's relationships. It's a uniquely human problem. It is saying or doing something that damages your credibility as a leader who cares. It doesn't take much. One ill-timed rant, one insensitive comment, one disrespectful interaction. The failure to be able to listen openly to the concerns of people because they "just don't get it" and they don't understand the bigger picture. Or just because you're having a bad day. As a result of our "rush to the finish line," a relentless drive for results, people you are trying to lead don't feel heard or led. You don't hear them because you're busy, distracted, you have important things to do and deadlines, or because you can't possibly be everywhere and talk to all of the people.

The truth is, most leaders try to do all of the right things to build trust much of the time (80 %). The problem is 80/20 isn't going to get it when it comes to trust. That 20% could be irreconcilable. I'm not suggesting that leaders can't make a mistake. I am suggesting they have to be able to notice (that's a skill) when they did, and they have to have people around them who they trust and who trust them enough to tell them the truth when they have missed the mark. Then they have to have the self-confidence to hear that feedback without making excuses. It would also be awesome if they knew how to prevent it from happening in the first place. The skill of self-control is a powerful leadership skill that needs to be better understood and taught to leaders. It's a total game changer. The biggest problem with it is everyone thinks they have self-control...until they don't.

Collaboration

There are so many things conspiring to prevent great collaboration in our organizations today. It's not because leaders and people don't want to collaborate, they do. Humans love to work together to achieve something great. At one point in time, it was necessary to collaborate just to survive. We are not the strongest, biggest, or fastest species on the planet, but together, we are the smartest. We know collaboration is smart and more fun...80% of the time.

We're back to our 20% problem. Because it's in those moments, when it's not fun, that the desired result of the meeting or the conversation can be compromised. Our leaders need to know how to get themselves and a team through the 20%. I'm not talking about constructive conflict; we all know that's healthy for a team. I'm talking about when it gets personal and heated to the point that the potential to engage a person in a solution is now very low. When a leader is inclined to get frustrated, to tell someone or a group to just calm down. In the history of telling another human being to "just calm down," has it ever worked? If we could teach leaders how to master those stressful or frustrating moments when things are not going according to their plan, and they knew how to swiftly and effectively redirect a negative conversation and the elevated emotions (theirs and others') in a healthy way, collaboration could thrive.

***

My views are not finite conclusions or ideologies meant to convince or convert anyone, nor are they meant as a display of academic rigor. It is more about the practical experience of being a leader in a normal day with all of the real-life frustrations and challenges that get in the way for even the best leaders. This book is an invitation to explore these topics with you, to see if we can make positive human behavior, under stress, a little easier to understand and more importantly to develop in our leaders. The examples I site in the book are real leaders who are all high performers, details have been altered to protect their privacy. They are courageous leaders and I have learned a lot from them

I believe that a new narrative is opening up about leadership because it has to. Never before have we needed more leaders who can connect with people and lead through the daunting challenges facing our businesses and our world every day.

I hope you enjoy the conversation and will start having more of them on this topic.

I'd love to join you and hear what you think.

Chapter 1:

WHAT WE ALL WANT AND WHY WE DON'T HAVE IT

*"Of all of the virtues we can learn, no trait
is more useful, more essential, for survival,
more likely to improve the quality of life
than the ability to transform adversity
into enjoyable challenge."*
– Mihaly Csikszentmihalyi, psychologist and author of
*Beyond Boredom and Anxiety: Experiencing Flow
in Work and Play*

Many years ago now, I took my then 18-year-old daughter, Danielle, to work with me for Take Your Kid to Work Day. She was entering college at Georgia Tech and going to study management. She knew she wanted to go into business, but she wasn't sure in what area. At that time I was in a senior HR leadership role in a Fortune 250 company. Although I had started my career in sales and marketing, I was offered a pass-through assignment in human resources. That pass-through assignment has lasted over twenty-five years now. I thought that bringing Danielle to work with me would give her a great perspective for what human resources work is and she could experience it in real time. I was certain she would love it like I did.

At the end of our day, I asked her what she thought. She said, "Wow, Mom. I kind of thought that once you got out of college and you were a professional, people would know how to work together and respect each other. It seems to me that it's worse than high school. You spend a lot of your day talking to people about how to get along. It seems like a lot of hard work!" Interesting perspective. I hope you're laughing now, because it is pretty absurd when she put it that way, right? What we call "breaking down silos," she identified as similar to high school cliques and people with different interests and perspectives not playing nice with each other. Not surprisingly, she decided to go into digital marketing! The work of "people and culture" is not the soft stuff, it's the hard stuff, but it shouldn't be.

So What's Up Now?

As I reflect back on that day and I think about the years since then, I can see Danielle's point more clearly with each passing year. I know that, as human resources thought leaders, we have all wrestled with how to drive engagement and build cultures where people want to come to work every day. Where people feel valued and appreciated. Where they know that what they do matters. As HR experts, for the better part of twenty years now, we've been deeply immersed in trying to train our leaders on exactly how to create those cultures of trust and collaboration. The data isn't encouraging. Why aren't we further along? I'm not saying that each of us hasn't had our individual successes within our organizations over the years. I'm quite certain that you have done some brilliant work. I know that I had a great team that did! I'm really talking in the collective about the current trends and the negative impacts work-life and culture are having on the people we care about in our organizations.

Technology

It would be easy, and fair, to point out the negative consequences of technology. As a result of our devices, we now live in a world that's always on. The vast majority of people check their emails 24/7 and answer them. We pick up our phones anytime day or night, weekdays, or weekends. And although many leaders may not admit it, not only do they do it, but they expect their teams to do it too. Over the past several decades, we have created a culture of workaholics. There has been a badge of honor in being able to show that you can outwork your colleagues. We all now know that we are literally addicted to our devices. Add social media platforms to the mix and we have the perfect storm. Not only are people busier than they have ever been, but they are lonelier and less connected. The sense that you can't compete or keep up with your peers has been drastically exacerbated by social media. High school and college-age kids are more stressed, anxious, and fearful than ever before and they are overwhelming the school counselling offices at every level. It's not just the kids, it's the adults too. Seventy percent of Americans are taking prescription medications for stress or stress-related illnesses. Technology has so invaded our lives and impacted our humanness, that before you can even log onto many internet sites, you first have to "prove you are not a robot." In his well-researched book, *Back to Human*, Dan Schawbel says, "When you replace emotional connection with digital connection, you lose the sensation of being present and the feeling of being alive."

Transformation and Change

Related to the surge in technology is the emergence of business transformations as the new normal. I can remember a time, and I'm sure you can too, where you may have had one big organizational transformation that lasted over a year. Where we had to figure out how to downsize fast, how to create whole new departments, how to eliminate layers of management, and, at the same time, keep the engine running and keep our front-line people motivated to serve our customers when they didn't even know if they were going to have a job the next week. We had our hands full then. Now this happens continuously. We are in perpetual transformations, a new one starts even before the previous one has completed. The ink doesn't dry on the org charts before we are in our "war rooms" drawing up new ones, and most of our people are exhausted by it. I believe this "age of business transformation" is a significant reason why trust in our leaders has diminished. People feel a constant sense of uncertainty and instability at work. Many people have not learned how to thrive, adapt quickly, or see the opportunity for growth in the face of constant change. Most people are simply in survival mode, including many of our leaders who are supposed to be leading the transformations.

Diversity and Divisiveness

As if all of that wasn't enough on the plate for HR leaders and business leaders to wrestle with, this massive upswing in divisiveness is piling on even more stress at work, at home, and in our communities. We have to figure out how to address and dramatically improve gender, age, and racial tensions at work. It's gone beyond just how do we get more women and people of color into leadership roles, now we have to understand how to restore trust and safety with each other at work. We seem baffled by the generational differences and "those darn millennials who just aren't willing to work hard and expect everything to be handed to them." Really?

The negative effects of all of the above on our people are easy to observe. I could quote to you from reams of survey data, engagement data, health statistics, and productivity costs the impact of all of this. I know I don't need to, because you have already read it all and you're well-aware. You lay awake thinking about it because it's your job to think about it, and because you do care. People are feeling burned out, overwhelmed, and frustrated. At the same time, in an unfortunate way, I think our people have become numb to it (like fish in water), having settled into the chronic stress of it with a resigned belief – that's just the way it is…live with it. I believe our leaders can do better, have to do better. We have to help them by deeply understanding the impact these massive changes are having on us as human beings and how we can learn to thrive in a rapidly changing world.

Turning Adversity into Opportunity

> *"As Patrick Pichette, Google's former CFO, puts it, when you have all of these factors in play AND a team of ambitious, opinionated, smart people, there is tremendous 'tension in the machine.' This tension is a good thing; if you don't have it you will fade to irrelevance. But, the tension makes it harder to cultivate community, and community is necessary to cultivate success."*
> – Eric Schmidt, author of *Trillion Dollar Coach: The Leadership Playbook of Silicon Valley's Bill Campbell*

Despite everything outlined above about the challenges we are facing in today's fast-paced world, the opportunities are even greater. We have seen unprecedented growth in our businesses, innovations unlike ever before. People are living longer, and the overall quality of life and potential for success has never been greater. Further, life on planet Earth has never been better. We take for granted how far we have come and just how "comfortable" our lives have become. Very few of us (certainly in this country) have to worry about survival anymore. Yet, we are battling daily stress and stress-related diseases at unprecedented levels. If we can figure out how to be that company that knows how to build resilient and happy leaders, they will create an environment where people can thrive and success is guaranteed.

There is only one way to do this and to change the tide of all of the challenges and stress for our organizations and our teams and that is developing leaders who know how to build trust and collaboration amidst stress and constant change. No outside influence can be brought in to do it for us. Our own leaders have to be able to step up. The story of Bill Campbell was written about in the book *Trillion Dollar Coach* because the leaders he coached generated over a trillion dollars in revenue and they credit him with changing the way they looked at leadership. People wanted to know Bill's secrets. Turns out, they aren't really secrets at all and anyone can do it if they want to. He focused almost exclusively on five timeless things: getting the details right when interacting with people in meetings and in 1-on-1 conversations, building trust, building collaboration, and love and appreciation (his favorite).

Keep It Simple

"Complexity is your enemy. Anyone can make something hard. It is hard to keep things simple."
– Richard Branson

We know that great leaders build great cultures and great cultures drive great business results. It's pretty simple. Honestly, as HR leaders, we bought into that a long time ago, before all of the research and data validated it. The question becomes, with all of these daunting challenges, where do we focus? What are the critical few levers we can pull that will have the greatest impact on leadership? How can we make it easier than we're making it? I have been wrestling with these questions for years. The only thing that has changed for me in recent years is my sense of urgency to do something more about it. That's why I'm writing this book.

Chapter 2:

MY WAKE-UP CALL

*"Tell me, what is it you plan to do
with your one wild and precious life?"*
– Mary Oliver

It was late July, 2012. I was in New York City. I loved that part of my job, getting to visit our corporate offices in New York. The energy there was so different than Atlanta. It was heightened and teeming with people of all kinds, which was beautiful to me. I was walking down Pine Street, having just gotten my coffee, on my way to work. Just a normal day, sun shining brightly. Then my phone rang and started me on a four-year journey that would change everything about how I looked at, well, everything.

It was my sister-in-law, Joanne. "They are telling me he has cancer, Jill. What do I do?" He is my younger brother, Keith, the guy that every family or friend group has one of, that last person you would ever think would get cancer. Keith was an avid mountain biker, effortlessly ascending and descending jagged trails in the Rocky Mountains on his bike every weekend. He was a loving husband and the best dad to two beautiful daughters, Brandi and Aly. He was that guy that everyone gravitated to, an uncommon mix of clear analytical thinker and contagiously caring person. He laughed easily, was equally competitive in all the best ways. Keith was master certified in LEAN by a Japanese legend in the field of Kaizen. Keith traveled all over the world to work with companies to, as he said, "help them get out of their own way." He said the most important thing he learned when it came to execution of anything was "Simple is better. Less is more." Most people think that Kaizen is foundationally about process efficiency. Keith's master teacher told him the roots are actually in "valuing human potential." This is the belief that it was unacceptable that so many hours of a person's hard work were wasted due to poor process and collaboration in hand-offs of work between groups. It turns out that valuing people's work also produces great efficiency and profitability.

Keith's doctors didn't give him much encouragement. He had one of the rarest of rare sarcoma cancers

(MPNST). Although they weren't saying it directly, the message was go home and get your affairs in order. But that's not how someone with his mind thinks. Remarkably, over the next four years (not four months!), Keith went "inward" to problem solve. He said that he had to know what this was here to teach him. It took quite some time and the most courageous battle I have ever witnessed (through more pain than is appropriate to describe here) for him to find the answers he was looking for. Once he did, he set out to teach us. He made sure that we (his family) got those gifts before he left us.

The First "Too Big" Problem

As an HR executive for over twenty years at that time, I was very "resourceful." I knew how to solve complex problems and how to find the top talent and skills needed to solve any kind of problem. I set out to do just that. I thought I was there to help Keith face this extreme challenge. As it turns out, I had a lot to learn still, and he was about to become the teacher, not the student – the one who would help me and, along the way of his journey, change a lot of what I thought I knew about life, developing leadership skills, and resilience under stress.

An Unlikely Source

I would have done anything to help my brother. One thing I did do was reach out to Dr. Jill Kahn. I had known

Jill for many years, casually, and I knew her incredible story of working with people who needed to navigate the utterly unhinging fear and complexity of a cancer battle. Jill's husband, Danny, was diagnosed with an inoperable, incurable brain tumor at age thirty-four. That was twenty-five years earlier, and Danny is not only alive and well, but thriving. In the years since helping Danny navigate his cancer, Dr. Jill helped thousands of other people face cancer head on and come out the other side. When I went to see if she could help Keith, she offered to help me. Confused, I asked why. Her response was, "You need to get yourself strong enough first, before you will be in any position to help your brother. He is in for a very tough ride."

It took me about three sessions with her before my leadership development brain was firing off. What she was teaching were skills everyone needs to have, not just people facing a cancer crisis. When I told her that, she said, "Yes, of course." Being a doctor, she had never thought it as a "leadership skill." Over the coming years, Keith, Jill, and I worked together to refine how some of her practices could be used to support traditional leadership development approaches.

Back at work, in my role as EVP, human resources, I set out to bring this work into my organization to pilot these incredibly simple but powerful approaches. Working with about thirty vice presidents, we piloted some new ways to build resilient and inner-directed leaders. It struck me how sometimes, accidentally, impactful innovation happens when you take a body of work from an unrelated discipline or industry and apply it to yours. The results of the pilot were extremely positive. We received feedback like, "powerful and life changing," "so simple," and "not only made me a better leader, made me a better person." We were told that it was helping our leaders think differently about how they approached everyday adversity and stress.

Mental Toughness and the NFL

During this same period of time, another accidental, or you might say synchronistic, connection happened. My son, Scott, is a professional athlete with the Premiere Lacrosse League (PLL). Although he is a great player, his true passion is leadership. He wanted to learn how he could up his leadership game for himself, his teammates, and the younger players he coaches. He jumped into this work with us and began adding many of the classic leadership and human potential books on my shelves to his own collection. His role as a captain of his professional team, as well as his Division 1 National Championship team, Loyola University, gave him a strong foundation of applied leadership experience, and his voice as a millennial was, in fact, unique and insightful.

Scott met Dorsey Levens, an ex-NFL running back for the Green Bay Packers. Dorsey is in the Packers Hall of Fame, played in two Super Bowls – winning one of them, and is a local legend in Green Bay. On top of that, he's a great human being. He became Scott's physical agility and mental toughness coach at the professional level. Scott encouraged Dorsey to meet with me. After coaching Dorsey around the practices we were developing, he said that his thirteen years in the NFL could have been so positively affected had he learned these skills earlier. He already knew that he was mentally tough enough – you have to be to play in the NFL. But he didn't realize how easy it was to lose his self-control and not be able to calmly and confidently stay in his own skin when confronted with challenging people, frustrating situations, or unexpected change.

I think professional sports is the most performance-driven business on earth. You get your performance review publicly from anyone who wants to give you feedback, and that's in addition to feedback from the coaches. As Dorsey said, you can get your pink slip by text message on Christmas Eve if you're not doing your job. It's a tough environment for leadership. The subsequent success that Scott and Dorsey had piloting this work with sports organizations further validated the potential to impact leaders in any business. Dorsey now visits clients in the corporate world (something he said he would never want to do) to help leaders adapt how they approach building trust and working together under stress.

Keith's Wisdom

> *"It's the simple things in life that are most extraordinary, only wise men are able to understand them."*
> – The Alchemist

There were many things that Keith taught us in his last months, weeks, days, and yes, even in his final hours. He was "holding life class" from his hospital bed. There were things he wanted us to know. I want to share just five of them that changed how I look at leadership and inspired my writing this book.

First, he became obsessed with joy. He would say, "JOY. You have to get people to wake up. There is joy all around you every minute of the day… you just don't see it. You think you have problems but you don't, all you have is opportunity." This message became a foundational concept of my work, that is understanding how to help leaders and teams still find the joy in their work even when challenges are coming at them.

The second was kindness. In his words, "If there is one thing, just one thing, we need more of everywhere, at work and at home, its KINDNESS. It's so simple; to try to be kind in all we do." It's so easy to forget, as leaders, even when someone's performance falls woefully short of expectations, there is still a kind way to give tough feedback. In the stress of our emotions, it's hard to remember that we can disagree without being disagreeable.

The third one was about seeing the bigger picture. He said, "We all need to look inside and remember we came to do 'heart work,' in the world, including in business." To support each other, to grow as people, and to innovate to make a difference and add value. We think we know this, but are we really putting enough thought into how, as leaders, we actually do this? We get lost in the complexity and challenge of the daily tasks and forget to see what we are doing in the broader context of being human and impacting people's lives and the planet. He said when you are facing death, everything about life becomes so much more simple. You see what really matters, and you realize you would do some things very differently.

Fourth was fun. One thing that he was so grateful for was that he had always found a way to love his work. He loved his team and his clients, and they knew it. "Work should be fun! It's about lightening up and creating things together, and enjoying the process, not just being focused on the result." Here's the thing, we take ourselves entirely too seriously. The pressure many leaders feel and the drive for results is causing them to lose their ability to know how to keep things in perspective and make it fun for their people.

One of the last, and most profound things Keith said to us was, "So much love, so much pain at exactly the same moment, how is this even possible?" In life, there are always going to be the hard situations but there is always the chance to see the positive even in those challenging moments. Then he told me, "Jill, not everyone wants to hear these things, you have to try to tell them anyway, tell them not to wait until it's too late to change how they see things." What people think are problems in their day are not really problems, they are just opportunities to grow and be better.

Ok, Keith, I'll do my very best.

The Framework

The framework in this book comes from and embeds all of these leadership lessons: simplicity, self-control, joy, kindness, and staying focused on the bigger picture, especially in the stressful and challenging environment we are living and working in today. In the coming chapters I want to share some new ways to put into practice seemingly simple ideas that can make such great impact when approached intentionally by leaders. There are so many useful skills and competencies we try to impart to our leaders that I believe we may be missing the forest for the trees on the ones that matter the most.

First, as leaders, how to be our best selves, especially when it's hard to be, because it's in those moments that trust is most often broken and when collaboration seems impossible. Second, how to connect with other people in simple but powerful ways, especially when they may not be being their best selves due to the stress and pressure they are feeling. Third, understanding how to lead growth and change by helping people connect to something greater than themselves on both a personal and business level. Knowing how to do this, one leader at a time, can build a culture of trust and collaboration. It can not only unleash creativity and extraordinary results, it's a lot more fun.

Keep It Simple

> *"Leading in a complex world means recognizing the simple things you can do to make things better."*
> – Condoleezza Rice

Chapter 3:

IT'S NOT WHAT WE KNOW

*"People need to be reminded
more than they need to know."*
– Samuel Jackson

You've made sure that your leaders have read all the right books, attended all the workshops, listened to all of the great speakers, studied the world's best leaders, taken all of the personal assessments; so why aren't we all at the top of our leadership game in today's world? Why aren't leaders prepared for the stress and challenges they face every day at work? What are we missing? We know more than we can do.

Have you ever attended an incredible sermon or inspirational speech? I live in the South, where we have those big mega churches, the ones with 5,000 people in one giant auditorium. You get in there and the place is rocking, the preacher is speaking "truth." You get in that energy and you believe that we can change the world! It just takes love and kindness and believing in each other and in something greater than ourselves. You are hugging strangers tighter than you hug your own spouse most mornings. You probably even shed a few tears as you feel hope again in this troubled world...we CAN do this! What happens next is actually pretty funny, if you just notice it. We can't even get our cars out of the parking lot before people are yelling at their kids to hurry up, firing off a hot email to a colleague, or honking their horn at the car in front of them (probably the last person they just hugged).

What's up with that? We know how we should act. We know our values. Still, we can't sustain being our best selves for fifteen minutes after we leave that environment and get back into our "normal day." We want to be the same kind person we were while we were inside the auditorium enjoying the sermon, but we lose it so fast when stressful moments hit us. Something as simple as traffic. The same thing can happen after a motivational seminar about great leadership at work. Most leaders want to be "that leader," the one everyone looks up to, the one who brings people together to achieve big goals, who is loved and trusted by their team and respected by their peers. The one that not only gets great results, but gets them the right way by living the values. But by the time a leader gets back to the office, they're hit with the endless to-do list, people problems, and too many priorities. It's hard to remember you came to drain the swamp when you're up to your butt in alligators.

So even though we've been building leadership content, engagement programs, and trust building exercises for decades, what we're doing still isn't enough in today's busy world. The stress levels and pressure are weakening even our good leaders. In a recent StressPulse survey by EAP provider ComPsych, 80% of workers feel stressed at work. The primary causes are workload (46%), people issues (28%), and home/work balance (20%). We also know that engagement levels are at the lowest they have been since Gallup popularized the Q12 engagement survey almost twenty years ago. We need to take a step back and rethink how we help leaders to rebuild trust and bridge silos while they are running the Indianapolis 500 within in their real day, not at safe offsites where the environment is set up for trust and everyone is usually on their best behavior.

Most leaders have been well educated. It's not about how much they know, the problem is they already know more than they can put into practice in their real day. We have an abundance of knowledge and an absence of wisdom about how to apply it into our real, everyday, hurried lives. Knowledge is complex and ever-changing. It's based in data and research, ideologies, and differing opinions. It's left brain stuff and we are pretty good at that too. Wisdom, on the other hand, is timeless, simple, and intuitive. For example, when we say to leaders, "People don't care how much you know until they know how much you care." Everyone nods in agreement. It's simple, it's wise. It's true. But do leaders actually apply that wisdom when they are in "driver mode" in a meeting and they notice that someone is in resistance (aka fearful) of the change? Are they trained to practice this bit of wisdom, to take the time to slow down and acknowledge a person's concerns so they know you care first? We have to make it easier for leaders to understand human behavior under stress and know how to navigate it both for themselves and their people. This is because behavioral changes love simplicity not complexity, so we only change our behaviors one tiny habit at a time.

Lemmings to the Sea

"To change is to think greater than how we feel.
To change is to act greater than the familiar
feelings of our memorized habits."
– Dr. Joe Dispenza, neuroscientist, and author of
Breaking the Habit of Being Yourself

Starting at birth the adults in our lives are training us on how to think, what to believe, what to say or not say, how we should act, and how not to act. Said another way, by age seven, our subconscious mind is programmed, and it runs entirely on habit. As adults, by age thirty-five, data suggests that 95% of what we think, believe, feel, say, and do in a typical day is based on habits/reactions, not on conscious choice or thought from the present moment of experience we are in. Our subconscious mind processes 40 million bits of data per second compared to our conscious mind, which can only process 40 bits of data per second. Our subconscious mind is one million times faster and more powerful. Think about that: one million times more powerful. This is why, even when you make a conscious choice to change something, like eating sweets, you often can't do it because your subconscious mind is not on board with that decision. You know there's going to be cookies at the 3 pm meeting and you just let your mind go on autopilot; what happens? You eat the cookies, even though you said you want to change that habit. This is also true for how we react to and interact with people.

As Dr. Bruce Lipton, Stanford University School of Medicine researcher, says, "The problem is that the subconscious mind is also dumb." It is governed by your amygdala, or what neuroscientist call your primitive brain, the part of your brain that sees only threats and is here to protect you. This explains why when someone is frustrated or upset and they say something unkind to us, we react as if we've been attacked and we attack back, rather than using our prefrontal cortex and pausing to notice the person is just upset, and we don't need to overreact. We need to simply understand what the person is trying to say and respond calmly. Do you consciously think of how you respond to questions when people catch you off guard and verbally challenge you? This "habit response," of the amygdala is a "fight or flee" option. Most often, we fight back or we retreat and feel shut down when stress hits us, even low-level stress. So how we respond to any kind of stress is a habit, and unfortunately for most of us, not a good one. We are simply reacting to whatever is happening in any given moment and we don't even notice it. We think it's just who we are, that's just our personality (or someone else's') and there's nothing we can do about it (or them).

This is simply not true. Robert Copper, Ph. D., a neuroscientist and bestselling author of *Get Out of Your Own Way*, explains that if we identify those moments when we react in a less than effective way to a specific situation or comment, in that same moment, we can interrupt our autopilot reaction and make a better choice and build the habit of self-control. For his well-researched book, *Game Changers*, Dave Asprey, the CEO of BulletProof Coffee, interviewed 450 high performers across multiple disciplines and walks of life to distill the statistically significant things they do that most people don't. Identifying and changing the daily behavioral habits that are less than effective to achieve the results we want came in third on the list ahead of education. We know more than we can do and only awareness and practice put together will change how we lead.

When I got married at twenty-four, my husband Randy and I bought a house and we felt so responsible, like real grownups. We knew we needed to make a plan for what we would do if there was a fire, so we agreed where to put fire extinguishers with easy to access from any part of the house, and we got everything in place. Perfect. Done. Then during our first Christmas, I'm in the kitchen and I smell smoke. Sure enough, the holiday decoration (the one with candles in it that apparently you aren't supposed to actually light) caught fire on top of the TV set. I run into the bathroom, grab a giant bath towel, run back into the living room, throw it over the flaming holiday decoration, open the front door, and toss the whole thing out onto the front yard. Randy gets upset with me and asks why I did that instead of using the fire extinguisher. So much for having a plan. If you had asked me, before that happened, how I would have handled that situation, I would've told you exactly which fire extinguisher I would use to put out the fire. Note to self: we all do less than effective things under stress.

The same thing happens all day every day; we're "winging it" and we often make less than optimal choices when we are frustrated, annoyed, or stressed by a person or situation. Lest you think this only happens when your house is on fire, here's how it plays out at work.

John is a vice president who is a really good leader (in fact, was trained and highly decorated in the military for sixteen years). His two direct reports, Dan and Elizabeth, have a breakdown in communication and they start attacking each other in an email to John. The two leaders have actually been friends for ten years, which is the first clue. John listens to them both rant about the other one and what they did or said that was "unacceptable." John, being a highly functional guy and not prone to either ranting or attacking people in emails, is at a loss. He tries to listen to both sides and figure out who was at fault and then negotiate a truce. His efforts fail and Elizabeth announces she simply can't work with Dan anymore. John sends Elizabeth to HR, which only exacerbates the problem and results in a verbal warning being issued. Now, back at the department, people are taking sides, tensions run high and productivity is suffering. The real culprit here is not that John isn't a good leader, and neither is it his team for that matter. It's that none of them recognized that the real issue was that the stress level in that moment exceeded the capacity of both of these leaders to consciously choose a better response. So, they threw the proverbial bath towel on the fire and punted each other out the front door. In the meantime, John is replaying the tape in his head for the next week and although he's keeping it together on the outside, on the inside his emotions are running pretty negative too.

Here's the thing, we could have helped these good leaders build the skills to notice what was happening in the exact moment that led to the blow up and how to apply some simple techniques to get in front of it. Any one of them, even without any help from the others, could have easily prevented this common situation (happens all the time in today's fast-paced high-pressure environment). Here's what happened: Dan sent an email to Elizabeth requesting another last-minute change to a deck for the client meeting in the morning. It was midnight on a Sunday night and she had been working all weekend. Elizabeth blew up and fired off a very caustic email to Dan which caught him by surprise. In that moment, he failed to notice that Elizabeth didn't really mean what she said, she was simply tired and upset. Had Dan been trained to notice that she was off her game, and this was an opportunity for him to exercise self-control, he could have decided to cut her a break and chose to offer support in that moment rather than reacting to her words and escalating the conflict. Had he done that, no doubt, after a good night's sleep Elizabeth would have apologized for reacting that way and they could be moving on. After later teaching Dan these few simple skills, he was able to repair his relationship with Elizabeth. As a bonus, he said he started practicing this technique at home, noticing when his wife or children were reacting out of habit to a stressor, and his relationship with them was so much calmer and more stable because he could consciously choose self-control and not reacting just because they were.

Here's how John could've helped his two leaders in the moment. As soon as he saw the heated email exchange, rather than waiting until he called them each into his office, escalating the feel of a crisis, he could have taken a more subtle response and called them each on the phone. First, he could call Elizabeth and let her know he's really sorry that she had such a crazy stressful weekend, and let her know she always has his support if the workload is getting too heavy. He could then have told her, "Hey, I've learned with my years in the military that stress does crazy things and sometimes it hijacks our emotions. I know you and Dan are friends, and I'd love to slow this down and help you guys give grace to each other on this one, you both deserve it and your friendships deserves it. What do you say?" With Dan, the conversation could be similar, except for Dan really could've noticed how stressed Elizabeth was because he knew she had already worked all weekend. If all Dan said was, "I'm really sorry Elizabeth, that was insensitive of me," it would have ended there. These really are simple solutions and simple leadership skills that could change thousands of these conflicts that occur every day.

Master Your Moments

> *"In reading the lives of great men and women, I found that the first victory they won was over themselves."*
> – Harry S. Truman

If you can master yourself (maintain self-control) in any given stressful moment, you can change your life and your ability to connect with others. Think about it. As we go through a day things can change from good to bad or from easy to hard in a moment. We get up in the morning feeling great, positive attitude intact, then our phone rings, "BAM," in a moment, "Are you kidding me? He did what? What's he thinking?" Our mood changes, we skip our meditation (or our work-out) and start making more phone calls or shooting off emails to try to fight the fire. We don't even notice that we're making choices in that moment, we think that we're just handling the problem. You might be thinking it would be a lot of work to train leaders to be this mindful and to stop and consider every single choice they're making in a day. I hear you and you'd be right! So, what if we had a way to know exactly which choices they need to make more consciously and what mental habits are getting in the way, so that it lowered the number from thousands a day to say somewhere around five to ten? We can train leaders with a few simple techniques to notice just those trigger moments that show them exactly which habits or reactions are holding them back and how to rewire their habits by exercising self-control in exactly those moments when it seems the hardest. We'll talk more about exactly how to do this in Chapter 4.

According to many studies, people will choose to change how they behave if supported by one or more of three conditions:

An epiphany

A change in the environment

New habits practiced daily over time

When leaders practice mastering their difficult moments by exercising self-control and their reactive habits, it not only allows them to feel more confident, it also helps others and it makes a positive change to the environment. It's a powerful way to lead by example in today's high stress work place. That's a leadership skill that will build collaboration and trust very quickly.

Problems as Opportunities to Grow

*"When we change the way we see things,
the things we see begin to change."*
– Albert Einstein

And a whole new set of possibilities open up. Einstein is referring to having an epiphany. Viktor Frankl, author of *A Man's Search for Meaning*, stated that very many of the patients that he saw as a psychiatrist, after surviving the Holocaust, visited him only one time. He explained that all they needed was an epiphany that helped them to see a new perspective about their problem. With the wisdom he gained from his experience, he could help them see how they could change their thinking and solve their problem. People who needed to do more work in order to change how they were thinking, but were not willing to put in the practice to change their habits, often never returned after the first visit.

Here's a great example of how an epiphany worked for one of my clients. Betsy, the general counsel for a large retail client, generally loved the part of her job where she got to get out in the business and work with the functional areas (like strategy). However, she was struggling in her relationship with the CIO and his team. She said she hated going to his staff meetings because all they did was challenge her and argue that she wasn't supporting them with the major contracts they needed with outside vendors. She said they didn't respect her expertise and she thought the CIO really didn't like her. It wasn't fun. I asked her how she felt when she was with them. Was she the same person she was when she walked into the room with her head of strategy and his team? She had an epiphany. She was acting differently simply because they had a problem and they were frustrated. She was taking it personally and becoming defensive and disengaged. She was not able to maintain her confident demeanor and work through the challenges. As soon as she realized it was her, not them, she went to see the CIO and hit the reset button on their relationship. They still had to resolve their differences, but it was not a problem anymore. She changed and then they changed how they responded to her.

Here's another example from a high potential Hispanic female client. She was seeking an executive coach because she felt like her career had moved fast for fifteen years, getting promoted every two years. She always had great bosses that supported her. Then it seemed she was plateauing at the Regional VP level. She wanted to get unstuck and moving again. She said she was afraid that her communication skills, specifically, her strong accent, had become a problem and she wanted to know how to overcome this race/gender bias.

After asking her a few more questions, I learned that she had a narcissistic boss who seemed to feel threatened and was always finding ways to put her and other people down. Apparently, he was a real jerk. She was in a constant state of resistance around him and starting doubting herself. I pointed out that she had never had to deal with a boss that didn't support her before, and that maybe he was what she needed to help her take her power back. The comment surprised her, but when she looked at it differently, he could be the "teacher" to show her that she needed to trust herself and learn how to navigate someone like him rather than lose herself. She had an epiphany. Her lack of progress didn't have anything to do with her accent or her race, it had to do with her own shaken self-confidence. From there it was easy to brainstorm how to deal with him and get herself moving again.

The first epiphany we need to have as leaders is how we look at the normal problems in our day. As Keith so poignantly said, we think we have problems but do we really? We need to invite leaders to a new way of thinking about how to navigate the stress and people problems in our fast-paced, high stress world of business transformation. Isn't solving problems what we actually get paid to do? Isn't it why we want to lead, so that we can bring others along and create new, innovative solutions?

If we are going to build this skill of real time mindfulness and self-control in our leaders, we need to give them the tools. Leaders and teams are running as hard as they can to get their "day jobs" done. Most don't have the time, energy, or interest to read more books or go to deep, self-reflective inner work programs. There is also still a large majority of them (many who are in the C-Suites) who are not super excited about becoming more vulnerable at work in order to build trust, or thrilled about practicing meditation to become more calm and stable. A good many of the senior executives I coach laugh when I suggest meditation. They say they can't quiet their minds for sixty seconds, much less thirty minutes. So, for them, it has to be easier. We have to meet them where they are. The ones that are willing to do deeper inner work will most certainly benefit, but that takes time and courage and we don't yet have enough leaders who are prepared for that. Further, even after people are brave enough to put themselves into those richer personal developmental experiences, they get back to the fluorescent lights of the office and the daily crazy and they often can't integrate what they learned with all of the stress and chaos around them.

So, how can we bring in some simple, practical tools and skills that will support any leader's efforts to build trust and foster collaboration immediately – and apply them right in the middle of the crazy day?

Get Connected

*"If your actions inspire others to
dream more, learn more, do more, and
become more, you are a leader."*
– John Quincy Adams

In the following four chapters, I'm going to take the highly complex subject of human behavior, or what I call "The Human Operating System," and break it down to practical approaches to better understand why we need to connect faster and how we can do so (with ourselves and with others) if we want to build 21st century leaders who can navigate 21st century challenges.

First, Chapter 4 (Lead by Example) examines how leaders can get connected to themselves. You can't give what you don't have, and you can't lead others until you can lead yourself. We all know this, right? Not new information. But can they do it in the harder moments of their day? With the people who drive them crazy? When someone dropped the ball and the client canceled their $1M contract? Do they know how to generate the energy it takes to perform at a high level throughout the day and still take their "best self" home to their family?

Second, Chapter 5 (Trust and Collaboration) breaks down how to connect to others. Specifically, how leaders can communicate across differences of opinions, ideologies, or competing agendas regardless of how things are said in those challenging moments. When everything is going great, communication really isn't a problem, nor are personality differences, or gender differences or race differences. We are all human and even when we don't speak the same language, we know what a smile means, we all appreciate a genuine compliment and we know when someone grants us an unearned "grace." The inability to know how to communicate effectively in those moments when we disagree or when someone else doesn't say it right, or when we feel unheard or disrespected are the skills I am talking about. Trust is not a character trait, it is a result. It happens by knowing how to provide safety and support when people need it most.

In Chapter 6, (Growth and Change) I'll dive into the biggest human motivator, the feeling that we are part of something greater than ourselves. So, in this chapter, like in the other two, we'll break down a big subject: connecting to something greater than ourselves. What does that really mean? How can we help leaders get connected to something greater and help their teams to as well? It's all about growth and change, both on a personal level and a business level. Today, this amount of change is overwhelming even for some of the best leaders I know. I'm not saying it's easy, I am saying, once again, it's easier than we're making it.

You will learn a framework throughout the rest of this book with lots of simple, practical tools, (and some humorous examples of how we humans show up when were confused and stressed). It is called "Get Connected." Each chapter will provide a different way to think about that specific opportunity to connect. At the end of each chapter will be an epiphany and one powerful but simple practice you can start using right now with your leaders.

Keep It Simple

> *"I'm a minimalist. It's human nature to define complexity as better. Well, it's not."*
> – Gordon Willis, director, cinematographer, "The Godfather" and "Annie Hall"

Epiphany

Life and leadership really is meant to be fun, otherwise, what's the point? That includes at work, especially at work, where we spend so much time and where we share our talents (make an impact) and grow as people.

A Simple Practice

Look at every problem as your opportunity to grow and get better at leading. Identify your unconscious/

reactionary habits that show up in stressful daily situations that aren't serving you, and practice a more conscious response. Build your self-control one tiny habit at a time.

Chapter 4:

GET CONNECTED TO YOURSELF (LEAD BY EXAMPLE)

*"If it's peace you want, seek to change
yourself, not other people. It is easier
to protect your feet with slippers than
to carpet the whole of the earth."*
– Anthony DeMello

I'm sure you have a leader, like my client, Suzanne, a chief marketing officer in a financial services company. She is brilliant at what she does. She has many of the leadership competencies we all use to evaluate top talent. The one problem is she can be intimidating and doesn't do well with people who are not as smart as her. When people don't do what she expects, she gets frustrated and they know it. She also moves fast and expects everyone to keep up. As a result, people don't want to collaborate with her. People don't trust her because she runs over them. So she got her 360 feedback and it didn't go well. She asked for specifics: "Who thinks that? What am I doing that's so intimidating? You asked me to be a change agent; I can't help it if there are some people that don't like the new direction." Her personality assessment says she's a driver and results-oriented, a good thing right? Even though she also got a long list of positives, she focused on the criticism. Almost all high potentials do. She doesn't say so, but she's actually confused and hurt. She doesn't really know what she's supposed to do about that feedback or how to make it actionable. She's working her tail off and is a high performer and now she's doubting herself and wondering if she should have taken this job. This is too common of a story. The names change and the specific behaviors are different but the problem is the same. We think it's a personality problem, but any personality can lead effectively when everything is going according to their plan. It's actually just a lack of knowing, as a leader, how to handle your own and other people's stressful moments, when things are not going the way you or they think they should.

A Whole New Approach

*"Between stimulus and response there
is a space. In that space lies the power
to choose our response. And in our response
lies our growth and our freedom."*
– Victor Frankl

I was brought in to coach Suzanne. Instead of focusing on Suzanne's personality "derailers" and her critical 360 comments, which were making her feel like something was wrong with her and everyone was against her, we took a totally different approach. We put her back in the driver's seat and helped her gain her confidence back by seeing where she was losing the ability to connect with others by using actual events in her day "real time." This way she could determine for herself, through direct experience, where she was not able to navigate her and other people's stress. What were the situations where she thought she needed to assert herself to get things done? She learned a new approach. Further, we told her that those challenging people that frustrate her are actually here to help her grow, if she knows what to do and how to stay in her highest power. I told her that those same people are going to be her best teachers to help her become an even better leader. One that everyone loves to work with and for. I could tell she was skeptical but she wanted to be that leader.

Here's how it works. The first step in this skill is to notice challenging moments in your day (going from subconscious to conscious awareness). The second is to choose self-control regardless of who is right and who is wrong. The third is to practice a new habit (response that you otherwise would not have done). Suzanne starts by noticing any moment in her day where she, or someone else she is with, is stressed or annoyed. Because these are the only times when we are likely to behave in a way that will that damage our ability to build trust or foster collaboration. How will she know it's a challenging moment? Simple, because it won't feel good. Her emotions will get triggered or someone else's will. Once she is aware of this moment, she's ahead of the game. The very fact that she noticed this is a challenging or stressful moment signals her to choose her next move more consciously (self-control) and will increase the chances that she will take a more thoughtful action and build that as her new habit. After she starts noticing how many times in a single day this happens, she will start seeing the pattern and how her less effective habits of interacting under stress are actually showing up so she can practice replacing them with better habits for connecting to others.

It gives her the opportunity to choose to interact with others in the most functional and kind way possible regardless of the difficulty of the situation or other people's behaviors. This takes leaders off autopilot reactions and builds better habits for how to deal with problems and people. Don't be deceived by the simplicity of this practice. In the first week, her eyes were opened, and she was actually excited about her progress. Almost immediately she could see how much more she was enjoying her job and her life. After less than two months, others were complimenting her and noticing too (and wondering what caused the sudden shift in her perspective, since her 360 was the same for two years prior and nothing had changed over that time).

Jill Bolte Taylor, a neuroscientist who suffered a stroke on the left side of her brain, wrote a book called *My Stroke of Insight*. In it, she describes how after the stroke she only had use of the right side of her brain. As a result, she did not have her reasoning and analytical skills, those left brained skills most leaders are so dependent on. She became highly intuitive and sensing. She said that when people came into her hospital room, even though she was unconscious, she could feel their energy, whether it was positive or negative and if it was negative (fear, doubt, or worry) it affected her ability to heal. After she remarkably recovered her left-brain capabilities, she realized that all of us can feel the energy of another person and if that energy is negative. One of the key takeaways from her book and her lectures is "Be responsible for the energy you bring into a room."

This skill of noticing, choosing self-control, and practicing taking responsibility for your energy, regardless of what other people are doing, is a powerful way to lead by example. Since we are powerless to change anyone other than ourselves, the best way to influence how other people act is to take 100% responsibility for how you act, especially in your stressful or irritated moments. Every leadership competency model has some version of "personal responsibility or accountability" on it. We can simplify what that means by looking closely at the word responsibility; it is simply your "ability to respond" to any situation. It's a choice, a practice, not a character trait. We know that the problems that are right in front of us will not get solved any faster by trying to control how other people should feel or act, but we still try! If we can train leaders to show up positively, listen carefully, help out if possible, encourage as many options as they can, make a decision when needed (after everyone feels heard), then walk away in the same good mood they walked in with, then that would go a long way to building trust.

Here's what it sounds like when one of my clients, Brad (a very empathetic leader), put just this one skill to the test. Brad took on a new leadership role where he had to influence a group of thirty-five other leaders who did not report to him. He was dreading how he was going to handle all of those personalities and heated differences of opinion. It was like herding cats and he was exhausted. He would get pulled into the debates, get frustrated, take comments personally, and try to referee other people's arguments. We talked through how to use this skill during the meetings. As an example, Catherine was one of the more vocal people. She always had something contrary to say and she seemed to need to be disagreeable regardless of the topic. He believed everybody was as irritated about Catherine as he was and he often would talk about her to others to let them know how frustrated he was (which only served to diminish his power and leadership cache). Before the meeting even started, Brad would already be dreading Catherine's behavior and strategizing on how he could manage her. His energy would already be spent before the opening gavel. I suggested that he start by letting go of the idea that it was his responsibility to change Catherine. (Largely because he couldn't, even if he wanted to! A great example of an epiphany.) So if that's not an option, what is? Next, simply notice (without getting triggered by it) exactly when during the meeting he became reactive to her. Then simply choose to stay in control of his reactions by choosing a different response to her than arguing, debating, or trying to convince her she was wrong (fight response of the subconscious mind). Instead, simply listen for an appropriate amount of time to make sure you hear what her view is, then thank her for her perspective and move on. No debate, no arguing, no problem. Two weeks later after just two meetings of practicing, he was thrilled. It really was so simple. He said, "The problems are still the problems and the personalities are still the same personalities, only now, I'm doing so much better! I simply don't get sucked in. I listen, acknowledge people's frustrations or complaints without taking any of it personally or feeling like it's a problem that there are many opinions. If someone gets upset, I patiently let them get it out. They usually cool down on their own if they feel heard. I quit judging everyone, especially Catherine, and I just keep the group moving forward by getting options on the table then making decisions." He told me he had been using the same skill at home with his teenage sons and rather than trying to control them, he controls himself, it changes the whole feel of the conversation and works like magic.

Mental and Emotional Energy

"All thoughts are good, they show you where you are in this moment and what emotion you need to shift to get to a higher frequency."
– Dr. Sue Morter, author of *The Energy Codes*

The key to connecting with yourself is to understand you are an ENERGY being. In the same way that all matter is energy vibrating at different frequencies. The difference between humans and every other species is that we have the ability to know ourselves as energy and to shift our energy at will to higher positive frequencies – as in better thoughts and more positive emotions. This is what I mean when I say The Human Operating System. We run on energy. Mental energy helps to form our thoughts and emotional energy helps to form our feelings. We also have physical energy and spiritual energy, more on that in a minute.

The easiest way to connect with and change our mental and emotional energy is to practice objectively observing our thoughts and emotions...and just shift them. First, we need to have an epiphany that negative emotions are not a problem. They are a warning light that we are thinking something or believing something that is depleting us. By doing this we are able to stop beating the crap out of ourselves and embrace our naturally occurring weaker (negative) emotions by seeing what they are here to show us and shifting them rather than wishing they would just go away. Here's an example: You get turned down for a promotion. How does this make you feel? Perhaps you start doubting yourself, or you start blaming the hiring manager, both of which drain your energy and don't feel good. Also, neither choice will help you figure out any faster what you need to do next to land the promotion you want. If you can notice that the negative feeling in that moment is self-doubt, right then you can choose a different response and practice confidence. By trusting there is something you can learn from it, you can then take a positive next step so you don't stay stuck in a negative state for hours, days, or weeks (draining your vital life energy) because something didn't go your way. Similarly, if you find yourself in a negative situation, and in that moment you observe (notice) you are frustrated, you can simply choose to practice patience. Why? Because being frustrated will drain your energy and will most definitely not solve the problem any faster. Practicing patience in that moment will cause you to feel more in control and to be able to think more clearly about the best way to solve the problem the fastest, kindest, and most effective way. You get the idea. It's less important that you pick exactly the right words to describe the negative emotion you are feeling. It's just important that you notice, name it, and shift it to something with a more positive energy, realizing the choice is yours to make. The more you practice (repetition) observing your thoughts and emotions objectively and noticing which are your weaker emotions that you need to shift, the more energy you will conserve and the stronger your mental/emotional habits will become.

Our thoughts show up in the form of self-talk. You know it as that ongoing conversation you have with yourself in your head…all day long, whether you want to or not. Once you start observing it, you will see that you are not very kind to yourself (or others) as the stories in our head are 70% negative. Just picture if we hooked your brain up to an electrode that transferred every thought you had from the time you woke up in the morning until you went to bed at night to an iPad where you could see every thought. Scary, right? This negative, very human experience is well-documented by our psychiatry, psychology, and neuroscience experts. According to research, we think 50,000 to 60,000 thoughts a day and the vast majority are negative. This explains the mindfulness/meditation movement sweeping the Western world and working its way into our companies in the form of "quiet rooms." Someplace where people can go to calm their minds and tame their stress. Not a bad idea. (Interestingly, many people think that meditation is about quieting your thoughts when it's actually about training your awareness and your ability to focus on what you choose to regardless of the negative thoughts that show up out of the ether of our memories.) The problem is you still have to return to the real world and practice something different in real time when those stressful moments hijack you, or nothing will change in how you respond to those stressful moments that steal your energy.

So, if you want to improve mental and emotional energy throughout the day, catch those negative thoughts by seeing how that they show up as weaker emotions. Then stop the story in your head, because most of the time when you stop and look at them, the stories we tell ourselves are not true, we make them up and then we act like they are facts, we choose to believe it. Watch how often you do this. It's hilarious when you finally see it. We are crazy humans. Have you ever done this? "She never answered my text from a week ago. I'm sure she's avoiding me. She has no right to be mad, I was only trying to help." Oh, wait, there she is…. She was on a cruise and didn't have cell service. Oops.

Here's how one client turned it around. Jaqueline is a senior partner in a consulting firm. She's a take charge person with an amazing combination of skills, a strategic thinker who can also whip together a detailed road map and implementation plan that rivals the most well-trained large-scale program manager. Effortlessly navigating from excruciating financial and technical details to abstract concepts and blue ocean brainstorming, she can be brilliant on stage in front of the board and can also communicate easily with highly introverted developers. She makes everything look easy. The challenge is her mind never stops. She analyzes (and judges) everything and everyone, especially herself. As a result, she is always in her head. She rarely can relax and is always afraid that no matter how good things are going, she's waiting for the other shoe to drop and something bad to happen. Not that you would know this about her if you met her. She seems like that perfectly put together executive who has everything under control. She's the type of leader who says there's no way she can meditate… it makes her crazy. I asked her to simply start noticing what negative thoughts or emotions showed up in her typical week, whether at work, in client meetings, in her car, at home, or travelling.

After one week of consciously paying attention, she said, "Oh my gosh, I had no idea just how often I feel frustrated or worried about something that I can't control or that hasn't even actually happened and how much of my energy it's zapping. Being stuck in traffic makes me so stressed. The lady at Starbucks who won't stop talking when I need to get the heck out of there and get to work. People who say they will do something then don't. My husband who can't seem to figure out what to do for dinner until I get home at 7 pm. Worrying about the bad weather that could delay my flight, but then turns out just fine after I stressed about it for two hours. It's insane and exhausting." Once she raised her awareness to these mental habits, any time she caught herself, she practiced shifting her thoughts and the negative emotions to a more positive frequency. For example, in traffic, when she would start to get frustrated, she would immediately choose to practice patience and pick a different response, e.g., decide it was a great opportunity to listen to that podcast or confidently call whoever she needed to and calmly let them know her situation without beating herself up. When the lady in the Starbucks started chatting away, she would just choose a different response and see her as someone's grandma who loved working there (make up a better story) and smile and thank her rather than judging her. Rather than get annoyed at her husband, she shifted her energy by thinking about what a great father he was to their kids, then just asked him kindly if he could handle dinner a few nights a week, to which he said "Sure!" Once she shifted her energy, she started noticing how much less anxious she was and how much happier people around her were also acting. After several weeks of practicing, she realized she was actually becoming a different person, much more in control of herself one tiny habit at a time.

With practice, you will be amazed to see how quickly you develop the ability to shift negative thoughts and emotions to a more productive and positive energy.

If you are interested in learning more about this work on a deeper level, look into Dr. Joe Dispenza's book, *Breaking the Habit of Being Yourself: How to Lose Your Mind and Create a New One*. Dr. Dispenza's research shows that if we really understood the impact of negative self-talk on our energy and our well-being, we'd work on reprogramming it immediately. You can also read Dr. Sue Morter's book, *The Energy Codes*.

Physical Energy

The next form of energy that makes up our "human being" is physical. Needless to say, innumerable books have been written on this topic by countless experts. But it is important to include it in this *Connecting with Ourselves* chapter. I'm going to, however, take this very rich topic and again, make it simple for your leaders so they can imagine themselves actually noticing something then immediately choosing one new practice. Here is a simple way busy leaders can quickly choose a new habit after they take stock of their physical energy. These are the six things you can pick. Even just one picking one of them will have an immediate effect on raising your physical energy if you are someone who takes your body for granted and ignores self-care.

1. Practice conscious breathing – any method will do, just notice if your physical energy is low and take 2-5 minutes to breathe consciously. Inhale for 5 seconds, hold for 5 seconds, and exhale for 5 second. Repeat 5 to 10 times.

2. Get more sleep, at least 6 ½ hours uninterrupted. Move your cell phone away from your bedside.

3. Drink 8 glasses of water a day – our bodies are approximately 60% water, it's our largest component.

4. Nutrition: Change just one bad eating or drinking habit. Get your blood work checked for toxins, micronutrients, and out of balance hormone levels.

5. Get outside in the sunlight every day for a few minutes. It's the most powerful energy we can access and it's essential for our well-being.

6. Twenty minutes of exercise 3-5 times a week (even brisk walking), preferably outside versus in a gym on a treadmill under bright fluorescent lights.

Caroline is a CFO of a venture capital firm. Let's just say she works a lot. She loves her job and doesn't mind the sacrifices she has to make. In fact, most of my clients really like or even love their jobs. She knew that her self-care was not what it needed to be, but she just couldn't make herself take the time. Have you noticed that when you don't take care of your body it whispers to you? If you still ignore it, the whisper gets louder until eventually it yells. Caroline ended up in the hospital on fluids for exhaustion. She didn't even notice until she actually passed out. You would be surprised how common this is. (Look into Ariana Huffington's story and research.) At the hospital, they recommended she go from 4 to 5 hours of sleep a night to 6 to 7. After her scare, she realized she could do that for sure with a little effort. She got tested and learned she was very low in a couple hormones and several key nutrients and found out exactly which supplements to take. For good measure, she also committed to take a morning break for ten minutes and an afternoon break for ten minutes and breathe.

Here's an epiphany: We can go weeks without food, days without water, but only minutes without air. What does this tell us? You don't have to be a yogi or decide if your belief system lines up with the research, just consider by looking at the obvious fact. Breath is life and our bodies need more air than most of us give ourselves when we don't do it consciously. Try the breathing practice above and just see how you feel after you do it. Better right?

These small adjustments can add up and it doesn't have to be complicated or hard, especially if you don't let yourself get overwhelmed by all of the data. I highly recommend Dave Asprey's book *Game Changers: What Leaders, Innovators and Mavericks Do to Win at Life* for some simple tips on maintaining your physical energy. He is credited with creating the word biohacking (techniques that the average non-medical person can use to improve their vitality and overall health and well-being) which is now actually in the Cambridge English dictionary. It has tons of practical tools and epiphanies.

Spiritual Energy

> *"Eventually, you will come to see that love heals
> everything and love is all there is."*
> – Gary Zukav, author of *The Seat of the Soul*

The last form of energy that makes us uniquely human is spiritual energy. Keeping to form, this is another extraordinarily rich topic which is as old as humankind itself. You could spend the rest of your life being fascinated by "who are we really," "what's our purpose," "why we do the things we do," "what happens when we die," or "where did we come from?" Not bad questions to ask, by the way.

That said, it's not my purpose here to suggest how a leader might think of expressing their spirituality. We have entered a new era where spirituality and quantum physics are finally agreeing on the compelling evidence that a power greater than us is the source of everything, including us, and, according to recent research, over 75 % of humans already believed that regardless of science's ability to prove it empirically. Take a look at Gregg Braden's body of work. He is a nominee for the Templeton Award and has written several books, including the *Divine Matrix*. He is a scientist and credited with bridging the gap between science and spirituality. I personally prefer to refer to this power as Divine Wisdom and Intelligence, our Creator or simply as God. Many people now use the words "consciousness" or "source energy." However you choose to be in awe of the force that created the cosmos and over 3,000 unique species of butterflies alone is entirely up to you. I will avoid reference to any specific religions to allow for everyone to connect spiritually in the way that best fits their beliefs. I offer it here simply because our soul is a part of who we are and it's the source of our creative energy and our ability to trust that we are more than our egos. That we are capable of far more than we can imagine, if we have the courage to get to know our higher selves. There are 7 billion people on the planet, no two have the same fingerprints, lip prints, ear shape, irises, or tongues. Seriously, we are also each only ourselves in ways beyond the physical, as it's clear that we each have a soul that governs our journey and creates our unique self-expression and gifts.

To me, leaving this out of this chapter about *Connecting with Ourselves* would leave out a critical aspect of understanding how to achieve our full potential or that of our leaders. Because as unique as we each are, we are also divinely connected to each other. We are softwired to connect with each other and to use the most powerful energy on earth, which is "love." This spiritual (versus religious) aspect of who we are as humans is likely the single most important form of energy that we can access and use to develop trust and build collaboration with ourselves and with others.

There is a company called Mindvallley. They are one of the most innovative and fastest growing companies in the educational services business, with online courses and live events with over 3 million students and counting. They have a "Love Week" every year that is one of the highlights of their extraordinary employee-centric culture. I think we could learn something from these passionate millennials. They recognize that empathy and genuine affection and appreciation can live harmoniously with hard work and rigor. They acknowledge that spreading joy, cheer, and positivity to the people we spend every day with is important – not just to be reserved for your inner circle of family and friends. During this week, they do everything from conducting random acts of kindness like buying a coworker lunch to leaving appreciation notes on desks. They don't stop there. They started a movement called #spreadloveweek that has spearheaded thousands of companies around the world joining the movement! How cool and simple is that?

In another great example of love in action, Jeff Weiner at LinkedIn has been a guest on Super Soul Sunday and talks very openly about building a culture of "compassionate leaders" at every level. It would be hard to argue with their culture or their success.

As a personal story, following a recent family trauma involving my son-in-law and daughter, I was simply overwhelmed by the unapologetic love my family and I received from my executive coaching clients. I already knew I loved my clients before that, but in moments of real human crisis, you'd be surprised how people you've just met or maybe only consider a "colleague" can show up for you. Relationships go from work to lifelong friendships. That's what love does.

Much is asked of our leaders. There are many responsibilities and many sacrifices leaders are asked to make if they truly want other people to trust them and to voluntarily commit their time, talent, and energy to the mission of the organization. I'm not suggesting all leaders would have to be willing to lay down their lives for their followers but many of the greatest leaders have done that. I am suggesting that if your vision is to bring people together to create a better world one company at a time, we could surely start with bringing love into the picture. Nothing builds connection faster and the benefits are too many to name.

Keep It Simple

"When you change your energy,
you change your life."
– Dr. Joe Dispenza

If I could only develop one leadership class from the thousands that are offered, it would be called "Lead by Example." Because I have observed over thirty years, and I bet you have too, that there are so many talented, smart, creative, results-driven, visionary, financially gifted, customer focused, and hardworking leaders in the world. Just look at the innovation, the financial success, the growth of some of our enterprises. Yet, despite all of that great news, people continue to report they are stressed at work, they feel disengaged, and they have lost confidence and trust in leadership. Just think what we could do to change the world if we could change that!

Epiphany

We are made up of energy. It is the fuel that governs our lives. It takes energy to live the big lives we've chosen and to effect positive change as leaders. Don't let your leader's drain their energy because they don't know how to exercise self-control and change the way they look at the daily stressors that are costing them precious life and leadership energy.

A Simple Practice

Take stock of where you are losing your energy – you may be losing it through your thoughts and emotions, or through physical or spiritual means – and practice one new small habit to reclaim your energy and vitality. Once you've mastered that one, pick another one. Keep growing.

Chapter 5:

GET CONNECTED TO EACH OTHER (TRUST AND COLLABORATION)

*"To bring some sanity back to the workforce,
it is critical that we improve our relationships
with our teams and build a culture of trust by
creating meaningful connections."*
– Dan Schawbel, author of *Back to Human*

The biggest problem we have on the planet today is the lack of our ability to build relationships and communicate across our differences. Divisiveness is on display everywhere you look. It's actually pretty hard to understand why that is the case when, according to Abraham Maslow, we all want exactly the same things. It seems when it comes to being human, we have far more in common than not.

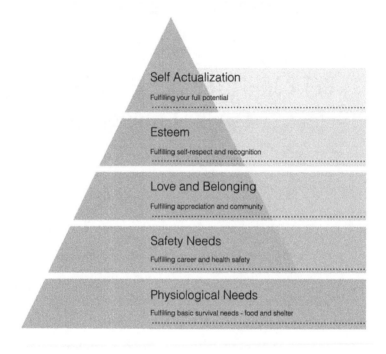

Self Actualization
Fulfilling your full potential

Esteem
Fulfilling self-respect and recognition

Love and Belonging
Fulfilling appreciation and community

Safety Needs
Fulfilling career and health safety

Physiological Needs
Fulfilling basic survival needs - food and shelter

Maslow's pyramid of human needs gives leaders a pretty good blueprint for how to lead their teams and how to build trust with people in their organizations. Especially when you consider that it's also quite intuitive, any leader can memorize it in a couple of minutes. It also would be fairly simple to apply to leadership communications. For example, if you are doing a business transformation that involves downsizing, when people feel threatened that they may lose their jobs, feeding their families and keeping them safe and healthy is all they are going to want to hear about first from leaders. When you are talking to that audience, save your big opening about the vision and why it's essential we change until you've given this serious attention. The next priority on the pyramid for connecting to your people is letting them know you care and sincerely appreciate them. What is so interesting to me is why we make something so simple so complex in many of our organizations, and even more curious is why we have to mandate programs to make appreciation and recognition happen. I understand the need for budgets for rewards programs, but appreciation is a "heart thing," and it doesn't require a budget. So, in the spirit of simplicity, this one is a mulligan. If you are a leader and you want people to trust you, the first and most powerful thing you can do is spend time face-to-face with them, and say, "Hi, I just wanted to say thank you and hear how you are doing." Wow. Done. So why don't more leaders do it? Why do we overthink it?

When we get to the top of Maslow's Pyramid, it's still pretty simple really – people want to have self-esteem, or said another way, to feel confident and successful. Which, of course, should be the number one goal of every leader, to develop their people and help them succeed. Something as simple as making sure you know how to give feedback (whether it's good or constructive) in a direct but thoughtful two-way conversation. Encouraging your people to pursue their career goals, even if it means letting them go to another team. Finally, people want more than anything else to know what's expected of them and what a "win" would be. I know, so basic right? Yet we often make goals and objectives too complicated and then struggle to know how to measure them. Many research studies done by firms like Franklin Covey prove out that if you pick only one big, compelling growth goal and take the time to articulate "From X to Y by when (date)," (using something that is measureable as "X" and "Y") for every functional area and team, overall performance almost always exceeds expectations in other areas as well, proving once again, less is more, simple is better. But our left brains hate that and we think we must communicate 5 to 15 key growth initiatives with multiple measures.

Lastly, the highest form of human motivation is to belong to something greater than ourselves, to feel fulfilled by pursuing a meaningful purpose. (Lots more on this in Chapter 6.)

A leadership class based on Maslow could be taught in fifteen minutes. If you have a leader who is trying to build trust and to collaborate with someone, take a few minutes and tell them to think about that person or those people as humans first rather than functional areas or job titles. What needs do they have? Do they feel safe with you or what you are asking them to do? Do they know you appreciate their efforts? Can this help them grow in some way or succeed? Does it connect them to something greater worth caring about? As leaders, if we get a little creative about how we can connect to our people and our peers, it really doesn't have to cost much.

The military sets a great example when top generals and other dignitaries put themselves in harm's way to visit a military outpost in a war-torn region. It speaks volumes about love and respecting their sacrifice. There are such powerful examples of what it looks like to infuse love into collaboration and purpose in the military. So, if you are reading this and you are in the military or you were, thank you for your service. It seems that some of our organizations have some frontline people who have been put through the corporate version of battlefield fatigue in recent years...give 'em a little love.

Relationship Rocket Fuel

BE KIND

BE HELPFUL

BE GRATEFUL

BE POSITIVE

According to a recent Harvard Business Review study, leaders who exhibited these four qualities were

40% more likely to get promoted in a two-year period. So not only is kindness a beautiful quality for a leader to exhibit, it also pays well! This would be another pretty short leadership class. (Maybe we need more leadership classes that could be taught in under five minutes.) This list would make a great addition to our leadership competency models.

It seems that even our bodies are trying to tell us we are built for kindness and connection. According to Simon Sinek, considered one the most influential motivational speakers and organizational consultants today, two of the four "feel good" hormones that our bodies release are oxytocin, which the body releases when there is love, human touch, and acts of kindness, and serotonin, which is released when someone is publicly recognized, applauded, or affirmed. Sinek also points out that another powerful "feel good" hormone is dopamine. We get a blast of it when we achieve goals – even things as simple as crossing things off your to-do list. That may be an epiphany for some of you as to why you are a prisoner to your to-do list. The downside is, as you may already know, dopamine is highly addictive. Another massive challenge of the dopamine hit is technology. Yes. We have become officially addicted to our devices. The formal name it's been given is Digifrenia. It sounds scary and it is. Every time you hear that beep that calls your attention or find yourself chasing texts, tweets, emails, likes, or Instagram photos, you are getting a hit. If you, like me, keep trying to deny your addiction, it might be time to start taking your power back by having some "technology free zones" in your day and on your weekends. Take a walk and leave the phone at home.

One last suggestion, when you go to have your face-to-face meetings to connect with your people, don't bring the phone – placing it in your purse so you can sneak a peek and placing it upside down on the table still count! (Yes, I'm talking to myself.)

In his book, *Back to Human*, Dan Schawbel also talks about the effects of technology on our connectivity at work and the alarming rise of loneliness as one of the greatest health risks facing our country. He cites Dr. Vivek Murthy, former Surgeon General, as stating that that the impact of loneliness on life span is equivalent to smoking fifteen cigarettes a day! People are literally dying for connection at work, at home, and in our communities.

If you want to have a pretty simple tool to measure the relationship connectivity of your teams, Dan also developed an assessment to measure this. You can get it at workconnectivityindex.com for free.

Best Bosses Ever

If you want to add your own reflection to the list of what makes a leader great at building trusting relationships, take a few minutes to do what I did. Think back over your career and answer the question, "Who were the best leaders you personally had and what stood out about them?" List any boss that jumps into your mind. For me, that's thirty years to consider, so I thought this might not be that easy, but it surprised me just how easy it was. I can still so easily feel their impact even today with such little effort to recall it. Here is my list. These were my best of the best. I thought I would share my own list, since, in some cases, it's a very overdue THANK YOU!

1. **Jack Little**: the owner of the restaurant, Weiner King (not making that up), where I was a short order cook and assistant manager back in high school. He trusted me so much. It made my parents nervous when I would come home after the night shift with hundreds of dollars in a to-go bag that I would bring back the next day for him to deposit! One thing that really stands out about him, in a way that is so relevant to this book, is that no matter how much crazy was going on, he never reacted. He was composed and polite at all times, never once lost control of his emotions. Considering the "people stuff" you deal with in a quick service restaurant, that's extraordinary.

2. **Greg Keeley:** District Sales Manager at Dow Chemical, my first job out of Georgia Tech.

Simply the nicest and most results-driven human you will ever meet. One time, he flew into Memphis, dressed in, I think, some kind of chicken costume to hand deliver a sales award I was receiving only to turn around thirty minutes later because he had to be back in Atlanta for a business dinner. Just one example of the powerful impact a leader's actions can have when you really let someone know you care and that you appreciate them. Much of what this chapter is trying to highlight.

3. **Mike Gilligan**: Senior Director, Human Resources at Taco Bell Corp. Mike was that leader that never seemed to have a bad day (and I know, there definitely were some bad days). His calm, patient manner, and the confidence in both himself and you was contagious. He was the "Lead by Example" role model for me.

4. **Pete Bassi**: CFO, Taco Bell, took me under his wing to mentor me when he had no need to go out of his way. I wasn't even in his function. I was in human resources at that time. He really made me believe in myself and my potential. He trusted me before I trusted myself. He was my primary client and I thought of him of as much of a boss as I did my actual boss.

5. **Regina Lee**: Former President, ADP. She never missed an opportunity to give a heartfelt thank you in special ways. When I resigned from ADP (yes, I was leaving for a significant promotion,) instead of walking me to the door she thanked me, with a Tiffany's bracelet no less! One I still wear today to remind me of her genuine leadership. She had such a tangible passion for people and for the business. She knew how to connect from the customer service operators to executives.

6. **Gene Mergelmeyer**: CEO, Assurant Specialty Property. He was my last boss (I'm my own boss from here on out!) and one of the best CEOs I have worked for and learned from. This is saying a lot, because over my career I worked for or directly with over thirty presidents and/or CEOs. Gene gave me freedom to be innovative with our work around people and culture. He gifted me by letting me be a trusted partner to him, which is what so many HR leaders hope to be able to do. Gene loves the business and cares deeply about people, not in the showy way but in that way that is authentically him.

Make your list and see if it inspires you! More importantly, see what about it inspires you.

Communicating Across Our Differences

> *"You will continue to suffer if you have an emotional reaction to everything that is said to you. True power is sitting back and observing things with logic. True power is restraint. If words control you that means everyone else can control you. Breathe and allow things to pass."*
> – Warren Buffet

Hopefully, by now, you appreciate that I am attempting to take massive subjects, any one of which have volumes of books and trainings associated with them, and boil them down to something you can grab easily and apply right away with relative ease. Here's the next practice for leaders to help them know what to do in those stressful moments when communications have become tense or challenging.

Dr. Jill Kahn says, "We never learned how to ask for what we want when we're stressed. As kids, when we didn't get what we wanted, we complained (or said another way, screamed, kicked, and cried)." Which, as many of you parents can agree, worked fairly often to get our attention! Now as adults, when we don't like something, or aren't getting what we want, we don't know how to simply and kindly ask for it. Instead, we use what I like to call "adult temper tantrums." You know what they are: intimidation, passive aggressive coercion, guilt, withdrawing (closing your door), being dismissive, hurtful comments, aggressive or threatening emails, and the list goes on. If we're being honest, we each have our personal favorite adult tantrum; you probably know yours. Mine is "the best defense is a good offense." It can be fun at times but in the end, it's highly ineffective at building trust or collaboration!

For our leaders, what do we do with this? Because it's really not a practical solution to teach everyone that you have to interact with how to communicate effectively when they are frustrated, angry, or triggered. When our egos get fired up (refer back to the amygdala in Chapter 3), we don't make the best choices. It's the biggest problem we have on the planet: communicating across differences (of opinions, ideologies, what we think we heard, what we believe, how we feel, etc.). To think that we're going to retrain everyone else is unlikely. I agree with Warren Buffet, it's up to us to develop the true power to know how to deal with other people's words. We need those in-the-moment skills and epiphanies to practice when someone "doesn't say it right" so you know what your options are that are better than reacting and taking things personally.

Like the examples in previous chapters, we'll use the technique of noticing, choosing self-control, and practicing a new habit exactly in that moment when you probably don't want to but need to! First, you have to notice that this is one of those moments and that something just got said that is taking you off your game. You feel like reacting. Before you do, pause and consider, if this person had the skills to ask for what they wanted more kindly right now, what is it they would ask for? Here is the epiphany: No matter what people are saying when they are angry, frustrated, passive aggressive, or just plain annoying, it's about them, not about you. Even though it may very much feel or sound that way! Once you choose self-control, you can try to understand what it is they really need or want help with from you. Then you simply reply as if they asked nicely in the first place, without correcting them or making them wrong. Help them if you can, if not kindly remove yourself and walk away without doing more harm. In other words, without taking how they said it personally. This is your gift to them. Why would you give them a gift when they're acting like a jerk? Because they are clearly stressed in that moment and not in control of how they're thinking or acting. Note: I'm not talking about those toxic people who are bullies or abusers. Clearly, interacting with them also requires a great amount of self-control as well as stronger corrective actions.

Let me give you an example from a previous chapter. Remember Dan and Elizabeth? When Elizabeth fired off her angry email to Dan about his insensitivity for sending her more changes for the morning when it was after midnight on a Sunday night? Especially after he took the day off to be with his kids and she had been working for the past ten hours! If you are Dan and you separate yourself from how she is saying it (remember this: when emotions run high, words lie), what is she really asking for? *"No more changes, please."* Pretty simple, right? She may also be saying, "I could use a thank you and a little support right now...I'm exhausted." So Dan, rather than reacting to her words, could have simply said, "I'm so sorry, those changes weren't that critical. I know you've been killing yourself on this. Get some sleep, I'll see you tomorrow." Done. Relationship crisis averted.

Another epiphany here is that in order to be able to do this effectively, you have to want to be that leader who is willing to do the work to help other people communicate effectively regardless of how stuck, mad or frustrated they are, even if it feels like they are firing their negative words and emotions straight at you. It doesn't mean you don't have to still solve the problems, you do of course. It's just now you go about it in a kinder way. You have to train yourself one day at a time to never, never, never, protect, defend, or justify yourself to others. Really? Let me explain. You don't have to. If you intentionally or unintentionally harmed someone with your words or actions and it comes to your attention (on your own or because you've been told), all that is required is a sincere and authentic apology with a promise to either fix the problem or do better in the future. Once you start justifying or defending why you did it or said it, your apology falls on deaf ears. If you are being falsely accused of something by someone (and I'm not talking about if you are in a court of law here) or someone is offering you that free feedback or advice that you didn't ask for, all you need to do is say, "Thanks for sharing that, I'll give it some thought." Then exit stage right without taking what they said with you, go on, and have a nice day. Leave their words with them. Words belong to the person who said them and not to who they are said to…choose yours carefully.

Keep It Simple

"Once you move one rung up from the bottom of an organization, the most important leadership skill that you can develop is the ability to communicate effectively with people."
– Peter Drucker

I would add…communicate effectively…*and kindly* to Mr. Drucker's quote. Keith's soulful and wise words echo in this chapter: "If there is just one thing the world needs more of, it's KINDNESS."

Epiphany

Our ability to communicate with each other really isn't a problem for the most part. We want to, need to, and like to be together! And we intuitively know how to collaborate, appreciate, and be nice to each other. When we remember to do it! However, it becomes an enormous problem when we can't communicate across our differences, and stress behaviors enter the picture, then almost 100% of the time the problem, whatever it is, gets worse, and goes unsolved.

A Simple Practice

Notice when someone else's words or behavior are rooted in a stressful moment for them. Choose self-control and practice not taking how they said it personally. Notice when you are in a stressful moment, choose self-control, and practice asking for what you want kindly.

Chapter 6:

GET CONNECTED TO SOMETHING GREATER THAN OURSELVES (GROWTH AND CHANGE)

*"The secret to leadership is simple: Do what
you believe in. Paint a bright picture of the
future. Go there. People will follow."*
– Seth Godin, author of
Tribes: We Need You to Lead Us

There are many sources of research from psychology to philosophy to marketing to brain science that validate that the highest form of human motivation is to find meaning and purpose by contributing or belonging to something greater than ourselves.

You may remember this from the previous chapter, it's the top of Maslow's human needs pyramid. It explains why businesses have "vision statements" that try to inspire and why literally thousands of books have been written on how to find your purpose. It is a fundamental human need. It also explains our rabid love of our sports, the intense loyalties to our favorite teams, and lengths we will go to support them. When they win the Super Bowl we do too.

Seth Godin, widely heralded as a "marketing genius," describes the shift that has occurred over time in what drives business. In the beginning of this century, it was scale and efficiency (ala Henry Ford), then mass marketing (still prevalent today), next, he says, will be the shift to communities, like-minded people who get together because they care deeply about an idea. We can already see this phenomenon happening with the support of technology and the positive side of social media. Said another way, it's what will fuel growth.

This is so important then for our leaders to really understand. I'm sure that I will "already have you at hello," when I say that the reason why business transformations have become the new normal in the past ten years is to drive growth. I'm also sure that you have been spending considerable time focused on change leadership as a result. It has been said that all leadership today is change leadership. It's become most organizations' number one competency on their leadership profiles. That said, it has also been widely reported that close to 70% of all large-scale change efforts fail to produce the desired results. Why? It's usually not the technology or the processes…it's the people.

Embracing the Unknown: A New Way to Lead Change

"The real challenge for the individual is to practice evolution, to learn the lessons of the old stories so we no longer need to repeat them, to remind ourselves that the critical mass of humanity involved with this evolution will change the world from the inside out."
– Dr. Bruce Lipton, author of *The Biology of Belief*

The way people talk about change is so often about "how we get through it," kind of the way you think about a dentist appointment. It's like pulling teeth and it's painful. We need to first change the way our leaders think and talk about change. The greatest two gifts that God gave to man are our ability to adapt to change and our ability to work together to innovate, create, and solve problems. Dr. Bruce Lipton is a developmental biologist best known for epigenetics, the science that proves that our environment affects the outcome of our health and well-being more than our genes. Said another way, we are always capable of evolving and adapting, with no limitations. This adaptability is stunning, really, when you actually stop and think about it. We should be fired up about it because change is required for growth, on a personal level and on a business level.

> *"The most important decision we make is whether we believe we live in a friendly or hostile universe."*
> – Albert Einstein

There is a young person named Austin Hatch. If you haven't heard of him you, you should Google him. At the age of eight, he survived a plane crash that killed his mother, his older sister, and his little brother. Austin's father, Stephen, a medical doctor, was flying the plane. Austin and his father suffered severe burns, but both survived. Within a couple of years, Stephen remarried, and Austin gained a loving stepmom and two sisters. Austin had a dream to play basketball for the University of Michigan. Despite his injuries, Stephen told him to stay focused on his dream and keep believing. By age 15, as a 6'6" sophomore in high school, Austin was becoming the athlete that could make it. The University of Michigan had reached out and offered him a spot when he graduated! To celebrate, his dad and stepmom were taking him to their lake house to spend the weekend and to celebrate. Unbelievably, tragedy struck a second time, and their small plane, again being piloted by his dad went down. This time, both his father and stepmom were killed. Doctors said Austin would not make it. He had severe brain injuries along with many broken bones and other internal injuries. The story could have ended there. It didn't. Austin recently graduated from the University of Michigan where he played on the basketball team. (They're pretty dang good by the way.) This inspiring story of the relentless persistence and faith that it took to overcome his injuries and be able to play basketball again is worth reading about. Recently, when interviewed, he was asked how he felt about his dad after two plane crashes, was he angry or bitter (yes, a reporter actually asked him that.) He looked confused and said simply, "I love my dad for preparing me to be the man I am and to be able to handle adversity and keep going."

The other critical part of navigating such difficult change and growth on a personal level, is to have faith that there is a plan greater than you can see from where you are, that God, the Universe, Divine Wisdom and Intelligence, human compassion, or whatever represents your belief in life, is at work in your life and for those you love. Not that everything happens for a reason but, that you can make meaning out of anything that happens. I can tell you, despite being a Christian, I'm not sure I would've had such a faith until Keith (not an openly religious man) made it so very clear to us that there is such a faith and such love right in the midst of anything we are going through. This is the link to your "spiritual energy" that we talked about in Chapter 4. I believe this is what Einstein was talking about in the quote above. Without it, personal growth can be a very hard ride and it can be nearly impossible to find joy and to trust your life when you are in the "valleys."

I share Austin's story to make a point about human faith and adaptability. We all know of famous people who have survived what were thought to be circumstances you can't survive and lived to tell about it (like Victor Frankl). What we often fail to realize is that there are so many more people that you've never heard of choosing to accept difficult challenges, to find the joy in the process, and to achieve great accomplishments by turning adversity into opportunity. It's a growth mindset and it can be taught by anyone who can model it (like Stephen, Austin's dad.)

The leadership lesson here is to keep moving forward with optimism and courage, no matter what hurdles have to be overcome with growth and change.

Change by Choice and Change by Force

*"The secret of change is to focus all
of your energy not on fighting the old
but on building the new."*
– Socrates

Life is change. Change is growth. There are only two kinds of change, change by choice and change by force. Both are hard, one is harder. Change by choice means you decided to do it. Change by force means you didn't decide and likely you weren't asked for your input. We all know that we grow from adversity. Yet, when we face it, our first reaction is to resist. We have to learn time and again that what you resist, persists. Meaning, simply, that the longer it takes you to accept the situation as it currently is, the longer you will stay stuck. Austin's situation was clearly change by force. He didn't ask for what happened; This is true of almost all of the biggest challenges in our lives. It is also true of the everyday, smaller but, still frustrating challenges that happen routinely these days at work in our constantly transforming businesses.

We think change by choice should be easy, then we are shocked to learn that's often hard too. For example, you decide to get married. Wonderful decision! You found an awesome partner. Two of you to share the joys and share the sorrows, share the workload, and raise the kids. Someone should tell us, though, that it isn't going to be all roses and champagne, right? He or she will disappoint you, and you will them. You will disagree. Your careers could come into conflict. Heck, he will want Chinese and you will want Italian on your date night out; It won't even be the big things, it will be the small ones, the everyday, ordinary challenges. We could just as easily substitute a work example, like you decided to take that promotion, and are looking forward to the challenge (not to mention the salary increase). Within a week in the new role, you find out your new boss isn't everything he was cracked up to be. The budget you thought you were going to have got cut in half, and your new team isn't very strong. You see my point. It doesn't mean that you made a bad decision, it may just mean the leadership challenge is going to be harder than you thought, and you need to up your game! Do you see it as a problem or an opportunity?

Let's talk about more about change by force. You've been dealing with this your whole life. You just never had a name for it, and no one ever taught you how to consciously navigate it. You didn't get the teacher you wanted. The coach made you move from the relay team to run the individual 400-meter race. Your boyfriend broke up with you. Your parents said "No." Again. Your boss didn't approve your request for more staff. You've been told, in fact, to cut people. Your company is moving the office to a new location. And on...and on....

How does this relate to being a leader at work? Two ways, first, you can't lead others through change until you can lead yourself through change (see Chapter 4). Second, as soon as you raise your hand to be a leader, and someone promotes you onto their leadership team, you have a responsibility to help them move the ball down the field. It's a leader's responsibility to get aligned and help lead change, whether they like all of the changes or not, because they belong to something greater than themselves. If you want to get to make all the decisions, work your way up to CEO and even then, the board has a say.

Here is a simple model that may be helpful for a conversation with leaders.

Here's how the model works. When a decision gets made by someone senior to you in the organization about a change, you may react one of four ways.

On Leading Change

DENIAL	RESISTANCE	ACCEPTANCE	ALIGNMENT
	Overt		
	Covert		

First, a leader may be in denial. It sounds like this:

Option One: Denial

Gary (the COO) decides that we're going to transform the call center including a new technology, using a new vendor that can help us scale. He's been talking about this for a couple years. You think they are too expensive and their platform is not yet proven and you don't like it. It will never happen. So you keep your head down and ignore it, you disengage for as long as you can.

Option Two: Resistance

a. Overt Resistance: "Gary wants to implement a new call center technology, I told him that's dumbest idea he's had and I told him why."

b. Covert Resistance: "Gary wants to implement a new call center technology. He's out of his mind. Don't you agree? Let's make sure that pilot doesn't go the way he wants it to."

Option Three: Acceptance

"Gary wants to implement a new call center technology. The timing couldn't be worse, and I told him that but, his mind is made up. I'm frustrated, but let's get the team together and tell them the news. The sooner we get started, the better. We have to make it happen."

Option Four: Alignment

"Gary wants to implement the new call center technology. It's not going to be easy, but he's very confident it will help us in the long run. Let's get the team together and brainstorm what the risks are and the path forward. We'll have to shift some resources, and we need to make sure he has all the information he needs before he does the negotiation with the vendor. This could be a game changer for us."

Can you see your leaders in these answers? Here's the catch. It's actually OK, initially, for a leader to find herself in any one of these boxes. Some changes are hard to accept and do have tough consequences on the teams they affect. What's also true though, is it's the job of every leader to have the open conversations with their boss, and then they need to start moving to the right. No CEO will be successful unless their team is behind them. The job is just too big. As a developer of leaders or a leader of leaders, you have to be very observant and open to feedback to see where your people are on the "alignment scale." If people don't feel safe or trust top leaders, they will appear to be on board but will not openly share this information, and it could be undermining your success. Further, your leaders have to have the courage to remove someone who is blocking progress for the team. The team will all know if someone is, in fact, blocking progress, and they will become disengaged if you permit this sabotage and expect the rest of them to compensate for it. This is especially true at the executive level.

One cautionary note: The only box you can't occupy as a leader is 2b. If that's you, and your boss finds out, it's an easy conversation for the boss. "I love you as a person, but, clearly, you are working against us here and that's not OK. I want to understand what's up with you and help you join up. I can't have you pulling against the team. This is a 'one strike' conversation. I'm here to answer any questions or concerns. If you can get on board, great. If not, it's probably time for you to move on. I'll help you."

You may be saying, this really isn't a problem for us, our leaders all understand the vision and why we're transforming. I would tell you to be careful not to believe your own press on that. Even when leaders understand the 30,000-foot level, there is lots of stress and resistance to parts of the plan and to colleagues in other functions. And that resistance is eroding trust and collaboration within your organization.

Rapid Rebound

> *"If you can control your mind better than someone else in that moment and keep your head in the game when things go wrong ...you have a huge advantage."*
> – Bill Belichick

There is a simple practice called rapid rebound that can help leaders and teams navigate change and uncertainty. Following the same formula from previous chapters, step one is to notice. What you are looking for is to recognize if the challenging moment that you are facing in a given day is the result of a change (either one you chose or one you didn't, doesn't matter). The epiphany that allows you to choose self-control and optimism, despite the difficulty of the change in that moment, is the belief that something greater is trying to happen. Then practice a skill we call rapid rebound. By accepting rather than resisting the circumstance (change) you are shifting your focus from, "Why did this happen" or "Whose fault is it" or "This shouldn't have happened" or whatever other stuck thought you may be having to: "What are my best next steps from here?" "How do I/ we move forward?" You don't have to solve the whole problem, you only need to take one small step in a positive direction. The faster you can do this, the less stress you will endure and the faster you will get back into a better situation. In addition, you will be demonstrating a powerful leadership skill for your team: leading through adversity by example.

Again, don't be deceived by the simplicity of this practice. Let me share a story and an example about just how impactful this can be, even at the most basic level. My son, Scott, is the head lacrosse coach for a high school here in Atlanta. Five years ago when he was twenty-four years old (a very young head coach), he was determined to get his team to the playoffs, something they had not been able to do. I offered to come talk to his kids about leadership. His reaction was resistance, "Yeah, sure, Mom, I'll get right back to you on that." (I'm sure back in the day, Einstein's kids weren't jumping on his program right away either!)

As Scott tells the story now (five years later), his self-talk then was, "Not happening, not bringing my mom into my locker room." A few weeks later, they lost a regional game that they needed to win to clinch a playoff spot. He told me they lost the game because the other team went on a run and his players folded under the pressure, got distracted, and started making dumb mistakes. Now they needed to win all of the rest of their games to make it. So, I tried again and asked him if he would let me come talk to them. He was a little more desperate now and I could also tell he didn't want to hurt my feelings. (I'll use whatever leverage I can!) I did have to promise him I wouldn't talk for more than seven minutes (the average attention span for teenage boys apparently).

I used an example of Jordan Spieth at the Master's the week before. He had one bad shot, it got in his head, and he continued to make uncharacteristic shots for him. Ultimately, he lost the match. I reminded them how common this is even at the pro level and that they aren't alone. Then I taught them about rapid rebound. If Jordan had been able to "stay out of his head" and finish the last five holes with solid shots, he still could have clinched. In that moment that something goes wrong, if you can stop the story in your head and focus forward, tune out the referee, the opponents, the stands, and just play forward, your body will do what you're trained to do: make a great pass or great shot.

Scott told me later that beginning at practice that day, anytime something went wrong, someone yelled, "Rapid rebound." Yes, it was usually one of the captains, because that's what leaders do. The more you can train yourself to rebound fast and just make the next small move forward, the more second nature it becomes. They used rapid rebound in all of their games to encourage each other when someone made a mistake or something went wrong. They won the rest of their games and made the playoffs.

Here is a great example from a client. Erica is a senior leader in a management consulting firm that helps their clients with business transformations. She found herself struggling as the firm itself was going through their own transformation. There were constant changes being made to every aspect of the business and to how she did her job that she disagreed with, as well as how she believed the firm should be doing things. She was increasingly finding herself in conflicts with her bosses and peers as a result of her resistance. I was brought in as her executive coach when she failed to get a significant promotion that she believed she deserved and that her capabilities and performance would seem to have warranted. The message was she was so talented and often the smartest person in the room but needed to stop fighting the changes and be a better collaborator. Erica loved the company and was passionate about its success. She was stuck, however, with not knowing how to navigate change by force, because she had strong beliefs and opinions and because her results were strong. Her stress level had become so high that she rarely enjoyed work anymore. Once Erica had the epiphany that she had to change the way she was looking at her role and that it was her responsibility for getting aligned with the direction (whether she agreed with it or not), she was able to start practicing rapid rebound in those moments when decisions didn't go her way, and she was able to move herself and her team forward. After only four months of hitting the reset button and building a new habit, she got the promotion.

Keep It Simple

There is a Native American wisdom about the buffalo. It goes like this. Out west, when the violent storms come over the Rockies, the cattle start herding and run away from the storm. The storm catches them just about the time they are exhausted, and many don't survive. The buffalo, on the other hand, run straight into the storm. They know their best chance to survive is to get to the other side as fast as possible.

Change is coming. Train your leaders how to embrace it, how to thrive in it. When you are outside of your comfort zone is when you grow. You will be surprised by the hidden confidence and gifts it brings you and to those you lead.

Epiphany

Most people say they don't like change in general. None of us like change by force. But the truth is that's crazy. Because life itself is change and growth. Every day is unpredictable, and we are not in control of what will happen. We need to see that if we learn to embrace it, and support each other when it's hard, the sky is the limit to what we can accomplish together.

A Simple Practice

Rapid rebound is a leadership skill and a life skill. The more you practice it the easier it will get and the more resilient you will become. Your confidence will grow, and life will surprise you!

Chapter 7:

PULLING IT ALL TOGETHER
(IT'S SIMPLE, BUT NOT EASY.)

"Yesterday I was clever so I wanted
to change the world. Today, I am wise
so I am changing myself."
– Rumi

All of Leadership Is a Skill Set

Leaders are not born, they are made. It's a choice. Let's just end the debate. The trick with leadership behaviors and skills, like any other skill, is that you have to practice them to get good at them. How many times do we decide we want to be good at something, like public speaking, so we attend a great class but then we fail to actually schedule and do at least "X" talks over the next ninety days? Leadership development plans are filled with goals and objectives around expected behavior changes that never see the light of day in the leader's normal day, and so they rarely move the needle and next year the same developmental needs are in there once again. Because, as leaders, we know more than we can do. "Cathy needs to be more inclusive and a better communicator with her peers." Really? The problem is, does Cathy know exactly what that means or when and how to practice that and with whom? After working with literally thousands of leaders, my answer is no. She doesn't really know what exactly to change, because most of time, she's doing the best she can. It's those challenging moments that are tripping her up and she doesn't even see them, much less think of them as an opportunity for her to grow.

The technique we use to wake leaders up to their higher potential and out of the habits of being themselves (their fragile egos) is three simple, but not easy steps. 1.) Notice those moments in your ordinary day when something is challenging you (or someone else) and causing you to react, to think, say, or do something that isn't going to get the result you want. 2.) Choose self-control. 3.) Practice a tiny, new, better habit (behavior) in that moment. Every behavioral choice you make in a difficult moment either brings you closer to or further away from becoming the leader you aspire to be. It either builds or destroys trust. The quality of your leadership, and your life as well, is the sum total of the choices you make in moments. If you can master your moments and your choices, you can master your life. I say it is simple because it is. It is totally within your control to be a great leader. It's not easy, because you have to overcome yourself and your current negative habits. That takes commitment, courage, and personal responsibility to practice.

Get Connected: The Big Ideas

The framework and tools discussed in this book are built around our ability to better understand how we humans actually operate and to see the opportunities for connection that can significantly enhance our leadership of ourselves and others.

Get Connected to Ourselves

"Our problem as humans isn't that we are inadequate, wrong, or broken. Our problem is that we believe we are. The fundamental misconception underlies every problem, dysfunction, and pain that we have. It can turn gifts into burdens, love into unrequited need, and a few challenging moments into lifelong disease. The good news is we don't have to live this

*untruth anymore. We don't have to keep telling
ourselves the same old stories about who we are
and what is 'real' in our lives. We can realize
and reclaim our magnificence and embrace
ourselves as the powerful energy beings we are
– and create from that place. We can do this by
remembering that we are energy beings, and
that ENERGY is the key to everything."*
– Dr. Sue Morter, *The Energy Codes*

It took me a long time to truly realize that I was the problem. That no matter how hard I tried, I couldn't control the circumstances I might find myself in and I certainly couldn't control other people. We all really do know these things, we just don't act like we do. When we get challenged or thrown in the fire, we use whatever means we have to protect ourselves, get what we want, or manage our own stress. We just get through it however we can and try to move on without seeing that it didn't have to be as hard as we're making it. We are definitely our own worst enemies and we have no idea most of the time how to stop the madness of letting ourselves, our circumstances, or other people drive us crazy! So the path to freedom starts with knowing how we humans are wired. We are energy: mental, emotional, physical, and spiritual, and all of those energies interact and influence us and each other. When we learn to harness and direct our energy to our lives in a positive and productive way, life gets so much easier and we can have a huge positive impact on those we lead.

Get Connected to Each Other

"Love is a word you don't hear a lot in business settings. Oh sure, maybe people will express love toward an idea, a product, a brand, or a plan. But, not to a person. We've all been conditioned and trained to separate our personal emotions from the business environment. We all want to hire people with passion, but only in a business sense of course, lest the lawyers and HR people get concerned. So what happens, what we live with daily, is an existence where our human selves and working selves are practically separate beings. But, not Bill. He didn't separate the human and working selves; he just treated everyone as a person: professional, personal, family, emotions.... All the components wrapped up in one.... What we learned from him is that you can't be one without the other. Academic research, as usual, bears this out showing that an organization full of the type of 'compassionate love,' that Bill demonstrated (caring) will have higher

employee satisfaction and teamwork, lower
absenteeism, and better team performance."
– Trillion Dollar Coach: The Leadership Playbook of
Silicon Valley's Bill Campbell

As leaders, our ability to connect with the human beings we work with and to build trust is the superpower of extraordinary leaders. You might argue that there are, and have been, some very successful leaders that really suck at that. I have heard some stories of pretty toxic CEOs running some pretty massive enterprises. I would tell you that in those cases, beyond what you can see in terms of material success, those people are rarely successful in the other areas of their lives. Further, many of them, despite their wealth, are not very happy. As HR executives, we know who the great "people leaders" are; it's pretty obvious. What I think we are missing is how to make great people leaders out of all of our leaders, regardless of their personality traits. So often we attribute it to personality strengths and derailers, rather than to recognizing how to help good leaders become great leaders by seeing exactly where they lose the ability to communicate effectively across our differences and in stressful moments. Further, if we can focus our leadership practices on the simple things (like those needs in Maslow's Pyramid) that help us thrive as humans – the things that bridge gender, race, and age differences – and remember how to connect on that level first, all of the other skills we teach leaders will be more valuable.

Get Connected to Something Greater Than Ourselves

On Growth:

"Wrapped within young leaves is the sound of water that will nourish them once they have opened. It's already there prompting them to unfold and grow. To believe that this is possible requires a faith in currents larger than any one mind can envision. But, that is not such a difficult thing to accept, for as dust owes its path to the wind, we, as human beings, are asked to acknowledge that something larger encircles us and prompts us to unfold."
– Mark Nepo

On Change:

"Life happens for you not to you."
– Byron Katie

We all do not have to become the Dalai Lama. We only have to believe that it is possible for us to grow and become the best versions of ourselves through adversity. When we do, as leaders, we naturally bring others along. Change is growth for organizations and for people. Learning to get out of our resistance to change and seeing challenges as a natural part of the growth of the business and of people is the first step. The ability to practice real time rapid rebound skills is a powerful tool. Developing our capacity to get comfortable in the unknown and to trust that there is a bigger picture, something greater that is possible, even when we can't see it from where we are, is life changing.

The Obstacles

I hope you will find some ideas in this book that will prompt you to take action right away. You are highly trained in developing leaders. You have spent many years exploring and testing new programs and approaches to drive positive culture changes that, in turn, drive business results. You likely have programs either in place now or that you are currently developing to do some of what I have shared here. I hope this conversation will inspire and encourage you to have a renewed sense of urgency. We all know that the state of stress and the lack of well-being in our country, companies, and communities needs to change.

I believe this skillset of building trust and collaboration is the difference maker for today's challenges. We all are craving it, and our millennials are demanding it.

They have seen their parents become disillusioned and downsized, unceremoniously "retired" after thirty-five years of service and they are not interested in waiting until they retire to start enjoying life at work. They want to work in environments where they can thrive and grow, have fun, and be creative and innovative much faster than the generations that preceded them. They can do it too. They have the skills, and we need to get out of their way and at the same time be able to teach them some things that only come from wisdom, experience, and age. It can be a wildly powerful combination if we can crack the code.

I'm sure from experience, you know that although many of the tools and practices in this book are intentionally simple and you can figure out how to apply them, there is also a great deal of real-life experience, study, and depth behind these principles and practices. I would love to brainstorm with you about any challenges you are facing to grow and support individual leaders or teams of transformational initiatives or large-scale change efforts. Just drop me a LinkedIn message at Jill Ratliff or email me at Jillmratliff1@gmail.com.

Chapter 8:

THE JOY OF LEADERSHIP

*"I promise myself that I will enjoy
every minute of the day that is given."*
– Thich Nhat Hanh

We are at the end of this book but, just the beginning of the work. My hope was to encourage you to begin a richer dialog about developing leaders who can be their best selves under the stress and challenges of today's fast-paced world. I wanted to share some simple wisdom, tools, and practices that can help leaders master their moments because moments are all we have to work with. I wanted to honor Keith by sharing what he taught me about what matters most and keeping things simple.

Leaders who choose to practice self-control and know how to stay calm, confident, kind, and excited about the future, even in the middle of the chaos of change, are worth their weight in gold. The benefits of taking this journey for them are huge: personal freedom, more fun, greater impact, and finding the joy again of being a leader. Eckert Tolle says, "Joy doesn't come from what you do, it flows into what you do from inside of you."

I believe most leaders want to be their best self. They just don't always know how to in today's demanding and pressure packed environment. They have become slaves to their to-do lists and the everyday problems and people that are driving them crazy.

They get lost, like we all do, forgetting what matters most in life.

The Daily Tempest

"It is a common place remark that our lives are surrounded with so much movement, so many pressures, so many demands, that our spirits are often crowded into a corner. As soon as we awaken in the morning we are taken over by the ruthlessness of our daily routine. In some important ways this is good. It means that there is a regularity and a structure to our days that make it possible for us to accomplish tasks which would be impossible otherwise.

But there is another aspect of the matter of daily timetables – an oppressive aspect. We are made prisoner by the timetable. We become busy – not the words: not, we are busy, but, we become busy. Within ourselves we develop an inner sense of rush and haste. There is a kind of anxiety that is like the sense of impending doom that comes into the life when the spirit is crowded out by too much movement.

It is true that for many people the demands upon their lives are so great that only careful planning in terms of a workable timetable can see them through. Even where the demands are not great and overwhelming, the economy, the efficiency of an established way of functioning, is undeniable. The purpose of such a pattern is not merely to accomplish more work and with dispatch, but it is to increase the margin of one's self that is available for the cultivation of the inner life. It takes time to cultivate the mind. It takes time to grow in wisdom. It takes time to savor the qualities of living. It takes time to feel one's way into one's self. It takes time to walk with God."

– Howard Thurmond, *The Inward Journey*

The Courage to Be Human

Human resources has gotten a bit of a tough rap over recent years for being out of touch with the business and for being too policy driven versus people driven. Patty McCord, who led the culture effort at Netflix, is a great example of a change agent trying to put leaders and employees back in the driver seats of culture. That work isn't about making HR less important, it makes what we do even more important. As human resources leaders, we need to deepen our understanding of what makes us all human, and then have the courage to put those things on the top of the priority list for how we develop leaders. We need to be willing to talk about "heart work," as Keith called it. When you really look into the research and the increasing number of practices in human potential development – like that of Simon Sinek, David Brooks, Brene Brown, Gregg Braden, Dr. Joe Dispenza, and many others – centered around how we create and use our energy as human beings, the data is fascinating. Here's a final epiphany to ponder; The electrical energy of the heart as measured by ECKs is 100 times stronger than that of the brain's EEG. The magnetic energy of the heart is 5,000 times stronger than that of the brain. So Keith knew what he was talking about…it's heart work.

It's such fun and fulfilling work to help our CEOs (they really do need us) and their leadership teams rediscover the joy of leading by knowing how to stay in their authentic power and how to help their teams do the same.

I wish you great success!

IN GRATITUDE

I would like to say a special thank you to Dr. Angela Lauria and her brilliant team for helping me make this book my "DCT." And also Thank you to David Hancock and the Morgan James Publishing team for helping me bring this book to print.

I am so appreciative for my HR team at Assurant. Jennifer, Jack, Bonnie, Libby, Kim, Sam, and Bob and the rest of the ASP HR group. They are the team that I got to work alongside (and made me look like I knew what I was doing) while I was learning how to be the kind of leader that I talk about in this book. Their incredible support, and their courage to be honest with me when I was failing them, gave me the chance to practice and to keep getting better. I have always said that if you want to stack the deck on success, hire the best people you can find. Nailed that one! I also want to thank my colleagues at Assurant, who both inspired me with their leadership, and who trusted me to help them grow: Kathy, Wael, Mike, Greg, Shaun, and especially my dear friends Peter, Gary, and John.

I would like to thank Dr. Jill Kahn for spending those incredibly rich but challenging years with me during Keith's illness and for her love, her wisdom, and support.

I am enormously grateful for my recent clients (and now, forever friends) as I have stepped out on my own, using some of these new perspectives and tools to see if I could positively impact leaders like them – who are already highly successful – to become even happier and stronger. You are all rock stars: Monique, Gabrielle, Alva, Kimberly, Angela, Tina, Todd, Brett, Sara, Bronagh, Avina, Lynette, Beth, Jennifer, Allison, Peggy, Tim, Maria, Kristen, Gissell, and many more.

To my amazing "sisters" and thought partners, what would I do without you? Joanne, Jill, Jennifer, Ann, Marilyn, Leslie, Jane, Tiffany, Tereasa, Mary, Helene, Latasha, Michelle and Lynne.

…And some awesome men, Dorsey, Jack H., and Norman.

Lastly, and with so much love: to my mom and dad for giving me the greatest gift of all…this life. And to my brothers: Kip, Keith (in spirit), and Kris, you mean everything to me. To my incredible nieces Brandi and

Aly and to Tom and Louie, my joy. And to the rest of my amazing family – step-parents, mom-in-law, and each of our loving clan, so blessed!

Ways to Learn More

There are so many brilliant people to learn from. I have benefited by studying the work of these gifted teachers, some still alive, some long passed over but still lifting us with their eternal wisdom. Below are just a few that I wanted to share if you would like to explore the concepts in this book and immerse yourself at a deeper level in studying what makes us human.

Spiritual Teachers

Maya Angelou

Dr. Michael Bernard Beckwith

Henry David Thoreau

Wayne Dyer

Joan Chittister

Abraham-Hicks

Gary Zukav

Dalai Lama

Sadhguru

Adyshanti

Paolo Cohello

Khalil Gibron

Rumi

Ranier Rilke
Oprah Winfrey
Eckert Tolle
Dr. Howard Thurman
Caroline Myss
Dr. Joseph Murphy
Mark Nepo
Byron Katie

Human Potential Development
Dr. Joe Dispenza
Dr. Sue Morter
Gregg Braden
David Brooks
Dr. Daniel G. Amen
Dave Asprey
Dr. Jill Bolte Taylor
Daniel Pink
Vishen Lakhiani
Brene Brown

Leadership Development
Simon Sinek
Darren Hardy
Sam Schawbel
Seth Godin
Patty McCord

Richard Branson
Jeff Weiner

THANK YOU!

Thank you for spending time with me and allowing me to share my story. I believe everyone has something unique to offer this world. I encourage you to trust yourself and put your special talent out there into the world. OWN IT so others can benefit from your wisdom!

If you are not sure how to take the next step to "Get Connected," send me an e mail address and phone number and I will do a free 30-minute session. We can explore any one of the topics below:

1. How to get you on track to get connected to your leadership potential.
2. Do a brief, but impactful, session about one of your leaders that you are trying to help step up to their potential.

3. Brainstorm ideas for a challenge you are facing leading the "people side" of business transformation.

In your email, just give me a brief idea of the help you need and your LinkedIn profile, so I can get to know you a bit before our call.

Talk soon,

Jill

Jill@jillratliffleadership.com

www.jillratliffleadership.com

ABOUT THE AUTHOR

Jill Ratliff is an author, executive coach, and leadership speaker. Prior to starting her own leadership consultancy, she served as Executive Vice President at Assurant Specialty Property, a $2B financial services organization. Jill has more than twenty-five years of Fortune 250 human resources management experience. She held key senior positions such as Executive Vice President of Human Resources for ING North America, Director of Leadership Development for ADP, and Director of Corporate Human Resources for Pepsi-Co's Taco Bell Corporation. She began her career in a sales role for Dow Chemical Company. Her strength is in making the complex simple and straightforward. Jill provides thought leadership and execution of "People & Culture" initiatives that align to and help drive exceptional business results. She has worked extensively in environments facing large scale transformational change.

In the community, Jill currently serves on the executive committee for the Board of Directors for Junior Achievement. She was also co-president for EMERGE, a nonprofit dedicated to empowering women by advancing their education. Jill has been a mentor for thirteen years with Pathbuilders, an organization that helps high-performing women accelerate their careers. Jill is a sought-after leadership speaker, focusing especially with leaders interested in taking their game to highest level.

Printed in the USA
CPSIA information can be obtained
at www.ICGtesting.com
JSHW082349140824
68134JS00020B/1979

9 781642 798593